Conspiracy and Power

Conspiracy and Power

Donatella Di Cesare

Translated by David Broder

polity

Originally published in Italian as *Il complotto al potere* © 2021 Giulio Einaudi editore s.p.a., Torino

This English edition © Polity Press, 2024

This work has been translated with the contribution of the Centre for Books and Reading of the Italian Ministry of Culture.

CENTRO
PER IL LIBRO
E LA LETTURA

Polity Press
65 Bridge Street
Cambridge CB2 1UR, UK

Polity Press
111 River Street
Hoboken, NJ 07030, USA

ISBN-13: 978-1-5095-5487-4 – hardback
ISBN-13: 978-1-5095-5488-1 – paperback

A catalogue record for this book is available from the British Library.

Library of Congress Control Number: 2022950230

Typeset in 11 on 13pt Sabon LT Pro
by Cheshire Typesetting Ltd, Cuddington, Cheshire
Printed and bound in Great Britain by CPI Group (UK) Ltd, Croydon

The publisher has used its best endeavours to ensure that the URLs for external websites referred to in this book are correct and active at the time of going to press. However, the publisher has no responsibility for the websites and can make no guarantee that a site will remain live or that the content is or will remain appropriate.

Every effort has been made to trace all copyright holders, but if any have been overlooked the publisher will be pleased to include any necessary credits in any subsequent reprint or edition.

For further information on Polity, visit our website:
politybooks.com

Contents

Who Pulls the Strings?
In the Depths of Intrigue

A few characters are strung together – and the message put out on Twitter spreads, rapid and inerasable, through the worldwide online space. Followers retweet it, and people who think it has a point keep it circulating. At first sight, it is innocuous enough: a tweet expressing a doubt, raising a question. '#5G Protect yourself from harmful waves and signals', 'Who benefits from mass vaccination? #Bigpharma'. Objections follow, replies chase it in vain around Twitter, while suspicion creeps in and fears build. Explaining the whole story is no longer necessary; a few keystrokes are enough to spread the word that a plot is afoot.

In the twenty-first century, this phenomenon has reached such vast proportions that there is growing talk of a golden age of conspiracism. Any unexpected event is sure to stir a frisson of distrust: environmental disasters, terrorist attacks, unstoppable waves of migration, economic meltdowns, explosive conflicts, political reversals. Amidst the confusion, the indignation, panic breaks out and the conspiracist fever grows. Who is behind all this? Who is pulling the strings? Who has hatched this plot? People look for the culprits for disasters, poverty, wars, inequalities, but also for countless abuses and oppressions, ethical decline, a diffuse malaise, a boundless loss of meaning.

Conspiratorial thinking is an immediate reaction to complexity. It is the shortcut, the easiest and fastest way to get to the bottom of a world that has become unintelligible. The people who look for plots are unable to stand the uncertainty, the open question. They cannot tolerate living in a changing and unstable landscape; they cannot accept its alienness. They are unable to recognise themselves, or others, in a world in which they have been left exposed, vulnerable, unprotected – but, for that, also freer and more responsible for their fate.

This way of thinking unveils, unmasks, demystifies. The all-encompassing explanatory power of the plot leaves no mystery unsolved, no enigma undeciphered. What had seemed unfathomable is finally explained by the obvious answer: a plot is afoot. *Here* is the solution. Bringing the world out of the shadows, it is possible to clearly distinguish black and white, light and dark, good and evil. Seeing things in terms of a plot provides a rigidly Manichaean picture – a reassuring one.

So, it would be a mistake to consider conspiratorial thinking as the quirk of isolated fringes, a subcultural craze, the residue of a pre-logical mindset or a stubborn superstition. It is not a regurgitation of the past that refuses to pass away, the return of an old spectre whose demise we can confidently predict. In this regard, it shows similarities with closely related phenomena such as denialism, anti-semitism, and racism. Indeed, we can say that this prism is a mirror of the times. Conspiratorial narratives enjoy such great success – have such deep influence on public opinion – because they correspond to widespread needs and stir up common aspirations.

A fringe phenomenon, albeit far from a marginal one, it draws in people who feel they are victims of both the chaos of the present and an anguish-ridden future. They feel condemned to a frustrating impotence, that they have been reduced to the role of mere extras in the 'games of politics'. So, while conspiratorial inclinations used to be something for aficionados, today they are reaching mass proportions; they increasingly appear as an ordinary way of being, of thinking, of acting.

The growing mass of 'conspiracy studies' in recent years takes its lead from research that began already in the twentieth century and has integrated its conclusions, developing them further.[1] The approach of these studies conveys the typical negative judgement on this phenomenon: their attitude ranges from good-natured irony to the most severe reprobation. There are mostly two lines of interpretation: conspiracism is seen either as a psychic pathology or as a logical anomaly. In the first case, this means plunging into the dark recesses of the mind, where a clique of microscopic neurons, ever-ready to plot, sets infinite traps for thought, pushing it to indulge an innate – and dangerous – disposition that risks degenerating.[2] Meanwhile the second approach takes us to the logic of conspiracist statements – i.e. to false and distorted propositions, or, in short, to the fake news propagated in the 'post-truth' era.[3] In both cases, these interpretations resort to a largely normative approach. On this reading, the alleged conspiracist is in need of cognitive re-education in order to correct the distortions in his thinking. Or else, his statements should be subjected to debunking – i.e. to refutation that exposes their illogical and false character. But, despite every effort, neither therapy works, and the wave of conspiratorial thinking continues to grow.

Such approaches understand this phenomenon as a problem of delusions or lies. But this demonisation is not just ineffective but counterproductive. As ever, the police-style castigation of thought, the denunciation by an inquisitor, serves little purpose. For some time now, an anti-conspiracist vulgate has been building which – asserting its own mastery of the truth – ridicules and delegitimises the theories it judges to be deviant, irrational, and harmful. But this polemical and pathologising approach, which vilifies any criticism of institutions, only hardens the entrenched sides and deepens an increasingly profound fracture. On the one hand there are those who are accused of being conspiracists, but who would call themselves opponents of the system. On the other are those who, as they draw on the canons of their own reason, are accused of merely propping up the dominant ideology. In short: a simplistic anti-conspiracism risks merely confirming the separation between 'official' and 'hidden' truth, thus preventing a proper understanding of a complex and multifaceted phenomenon.

Conspiracism is neither an intellectual barrier nor a fallacious argument. Rather, it is a political problem. It is not so much about truth as it is about power. It is strange that, despite the wide-ranging reflection on this problem, the decisive tangle has not been unravelled: the one that ties power to the work of the plot.

Those who challenge the official version of events aim to attack the bearers of knowledge and power. Their distrust of politics, institutions, the media, experts, becomes systematic dissatisfaction and boundless suspicion. If under the polluted skies of globalisation, catastrophic events are multiplying, and if the world seems doomed to unstoppable chaos, this must be because of the 'caste', the 'oligarchy', 'international finance'. It is, then, necessary to have sharper eyes and unmask the hidden plans of the 'New World Order'. But what kind of revolt is even possible against this kind of faceless power? The tacit admission of this powerlessness goes hand in hand with a sullen *ressentiment*, an explosive rage and the urgent need to unveil The Plot that has spun its threads around power. In the conspiracist hall of mirrors, it is always *others* who are working up plots, while those who level the accusations are only seeking to defend themselves. The 'occult powers', the 'real powers that be',[4] are called into question by a political theory that sees governance as a plot and thus advocates a strategy and practice of counter-power necessarily understood as a counter-plot. It would seem the 'little people' have no other form of resistance against the 'masters of the world'.

Conspiracism expresses a widespread malaise and manifests a deep unease. It is not merely a marker of obscurantism, but it surely is a dark sign. It exposes the crisis that is convulsing contemporary democracy. Just think of all the broken promises! All the betrayed hopes! And what does the word 'democracy' even mean, if not the long-awaited 'government of, by, for the people'? Yet – as if through some cruel joke – the sovereign people do not really feel sovereign. Power seems to elude them, threatened by the uncontrollable power of The Plot. This is not just a suspicion. Democratic power seems like an illusion. Governments come and go, parties exchange the reins of office between themselves, but nothing really changes. What remains is the 'Deep State', the institutional power kept intact and perpetuated by castes, lobbies, banks, dynasties, and media moguls. It may be more or less of a secret, but it's they who are pulling the strings – that's the foundation, the principle of real power!

But the fact that in recent times presidents and heads of government have pointed the finger at the Deep State and cried 'conspiracy!' ought to give pause for thought. When they do this, it is not just a ploy to shake off any responsibility for governing, and nor is it just a geopolitical defence move. Reference to the 'Deep State' has become a catchphrase that, in its own insidious way, confirms what a dismal condition enthusiasm for democracy has fallen into. It insinuates that democracy has been hollowed of all value – that it is, indeed, a mere 'farce'. Here, conspiracist doubts converge with a certain populist vision of popular sovereignty, reduced to a simulacrum by the 'real powers that be'.

Is it possible that democracy is just what it appears to be? The empty space of democratic power seems just too empty. Conspiracism renders the archaic idea of an absolute power incompatible with democracy. But perhaps The Plot is precisely the mask that power puts on in an age of faceless power. So, it is instead necessary to unmask the archaic mechanism that drives people to hypothesise an *arché* – a principle and a command – which democracy ought to have deposed long ago.

Politics and its Shadow-Realm

Millions of people around the world believe that politicians are mere puppets whose strings are pulled by occult forces. All is not as it seems. Behind the apparent but deceptive reality lies a more authentic, truer one. This splitting of reality, this dichotomy between outside and inside, surface and depth – almost reminiscent of Plato's myth of the cave – is characteristic of the contemporary metaphysics of politics.

If the individuals operating in the shadow-realm that gets passed off as reality are manipulated puppets, merely illusory simulacra, then we must also ask where the puppeteers are hiding. Who is behind it all? Who rules the rulers? Who pulls the strings?

These questions, which already openly allude to The Plot, direct suspicions towards the locus of power and the foundation of authority. But, above all, this is about ascertaining who really has power. Perhaps the men and women called on to serve a term in office? Or those in other posts behind the scenes, who have much more room for manoeuvre, since they don't have to account for the consequences? As reality splits in two, a gap emerges between official and unofficial power – the recognised but fictitious power, and the illegitimate but real one. It is said that, behind the façade of external reality, with its hierarchies, relation-ships, and principles, at which the naive gaze stops, there is concealed another, more real and threatening reality, inhabited by a power whose existence no one suspects or, rather, of which no one can even imagine the possibility. This is the field of operation of individuals and groups held together by family ties, personal relationships, economic interests, and political aspirations. Such connivance, which has no legal expression, is the mutual support, the aiding and abetting – the averted gaze which nods along – in the exercise of power. It is in this hidden realm, amidst the pulled strings, the webs and ties, that the plot takes shape.

What are the forces that govern the nation? Which ones direct the market? What face do the masters of the world have? Who determines the course of history? There is a search to find who is responsible for the countless intrigues: is it bankers, financiers, capitalists, or anarchists, subversives, terrorists, or even Jews, internationalists, cos-mopolitans, foreign powers? Many alternatives can be speculated upon.

What is certain is that the idea that there are plots is itself thriving. Far from being a niche phenomenon, it appears as a global one, indeed one with mass dimen-sions. Conspiracist narratives are now established in the public sphere. They cannot be considered, as an old stere-otype would have it, an idiosyncratic product of extremist fringes. Rather, they constitute the kaleidoscope through which the events of the world are read by the majority. No one seems to escape them.

There is a long history of such theories, and we could cite countless examples of them. The most emblematic, if we look at the recent past, was and is the assassination of John Fitzgerald Kennedy: the vast majority do not believe the 'official version' and cling to the belief that he was the victim of some sort of plot. Oswald could not have been the only shooter. The KKK, the Mafia, the CIA must have been involved. This intelligence agency – a malignant expression of US power – has long been the ideal culprit; its acronym is the seal with which any investigation is at least provisionally closed. In some cases, even time does not help to dispel doubts. Thus, more and more people around the world believe that the 9/11 attacks were the result of a well-orchestrated 'inside job', with the direct involvement of the Bush administration. The list of conspiracies could go on. The Apollo 11 moon landing was filmed on a TV set; climate change is a hoax by scientists; Barack Obama is a socialist Muslim from Kenya; George Soros spearheads the Kalergi Plan for the 'ethnic replacement' of European peoples; the Sars-CoV-2 coronavirus, cooked up at the Wuhan Institute of Virology, is a Chinese-made biological weapon; vaccines are themselves to be feared because they cause diseases such as autism. Big Pharma's plots are a constant source of apprehension, while the shadowy set-ups of the 'New World Order' sow disquiet.

Traces of the plot can be found everywhere: in the air we breathe, poisoned by chemtrails, in the water we drink, spiked with fluorides, in the earth polluted beyond repair. And there is also a plot to be uncovered in the traces and clues that remain undeciphered, in the past as in the future. What is generally believed is only a lie, while the truth lies somewhere else. In short, history must also be re-read, to unmask the plots that are still at work in the present. And the biggest, most successful deception – we know – is still the great 'myth' that Adolf Hitler killed six million Jews.

Conspiracism extends from the furthest shores of the far right to the most unlikely parts of the left. But, beyond political life, it is difficult to find an area immune to the conspiracist contagion: from economic governance to health issues, from the scientific context to the ecclesiastical universe, not to mention history. The enormous spread of conspiracism, also bolstered by the proliferation of fake news, is attested by books, essays, articles, films, television series, historical documentaries, and journalistic investigations, where often even the most careful analyses end up mixing fiction with reality. The conspiracy industry can boast successes that have swept around the planet, such as the *Matrix* films – themselves subject to widespread commentary – or the *X-Files*, but also bestsellers such as Dan Brown's *The Da Vinci Code*, which draws on old antisemitic stereotypes while edulcorating them in the form of a fictional saga. The interest in conspiracist themes thus extends beyond the frontiers of the considerable literature on this genre – that is, both books providing evidence and counter-evidence on single events and collections of the most famous conspiracies.[1] We can explain its spread in terms of a real game of mirrors, a circular effect, spurred on by the proliferation of media and the unlimited space of the web, where conspiracist ideas spread like wildfire. Here is the realm of media nihilism, where everyone believes anything and no one believes anything any more.

The Unreadability of the World

For some time now, the planetary space has offered the spectacle of a disturbing chaos. Profound upheavals, rapid changes, and unforeseen developments mark the accelerated pace of an era which – while it promised to be clear and distinct, indeed transparent – instead appears in all its scandalous opacity.

The world engulfed by capital, characterised by boundless debt and yawning inequalities, is an unstable and confused landscape, riven by regurgitations of anger and unsettled by a diffuse hostility. Spectral peace slips into endemic war, friend is no longer distinguished from enemy, every face resembles a mask and everything seems to take place under a false flag.

It is the age of uncertainty. There is growing fear over the many new threats, growing anxiety over the incomprehensible events that threaten to divert the course of history, increasing distress at the signs of catastrophe. Confidence is shaken. Initial bewilderment is replaced by an icy indignation. In its unbearable absurdity, what is happening defies all understanding.

The world appears unreadable. Its grammar is abstruse,

its syntax elusive. It is as if it were no longer possible to recover the internal connections, the links that previously seemed to bind the whole together. The mythical ancient thread, the one Ariadne gave Theseus to find his way through the labyrinth, has frayed – indeed, it has broken forever. But the contemporary drama has a paradoxical trait, because Theseus no longer recognises the traces he has left behind him. It is almost as if, after the long wanderings, the path has become so complex that it can hardly be retraced. It is no longer nature that is impenetrable. Rather, human history has itself become enigmatic.

This has happened precisely at the height of globalisation, at a time when the world – conquered, anthropised, technologised – had seemed to become available, within reach. The human subject contemplated the world in front of him and forged his own worldview, believing that he recognised himself and his own history.

But suddenly the subject who considered himself master of the world, the privileged centre of the system, putting his frame on its patterns, can no longer find his bearings. He is lost. The connections have vanished. The overall vision disintegrates. The designer suspects the design has been set out on his behalf. The manoeuvrer feels manoeuvred.

The great Book of History is now indecipherable. The legibility of the world, emphasised by so many philosophers from Vico to Blumenberg, seems to be just a mirage. We can no longer read what we ourselves have written. Deterioration, wear and tear, simulation and deception hinder reading, prevent exegesis. This is not a question of the variety of interpretations, itself inevitable. It is that the world has unravelled. It no longer unfolds, starting from that shared Book, in accordance with a shared sense of meaning.

The thread of the narrative has broken, the pattern has been torn apart. All that remains is an intrigue that is difficult to unravel. And yet, there must be knots that still maintain the warp of the fabric, the hidden links that tie together the whole. All we need is to look for them.

The world has a hidden side, a netherworld, a secret realm, teeming with clandestine activities and covert operations. It is there that plans are being hatched, information is manipulated, thoughts are controlled, and convictions are forged. There, in that occult intrigue, hold firm the threads of a pattern which appears frayed only from the outside. As if by magic, the world which can now be brought out of the shadow-realm seems lit up by an unprecedented glow. Everything finally fits together. Everything has a firm foundation and a precise cause again. The *chiaroscuro* of global disorder is banished, its darkness instead traced back to the 'dark forces' at work in the netherworld. Everything becomes legible again, through the prism of The Plot.

The chaotic world suddenly takes on firm and sharp contours. It is possible to stitch together the fabric of the narrative, to restore the order of interpretation. Even those who considered their lives isolated, dispersed, so unjustly consigned to oblivion, so terribly disconnected from the life of the world, of which it was but an ephemeral episode, regain their bearings. The idea of the plot re-establishes a link – however imaginary – with other lives and with History itself. Here, then, is a way to get a handle on the future, whose linear development now again appears intact. It is possible to give a global, overall meaning to events again.

Conspiracists are nostalgic for legibility. They harbour the illusion of being able to explain everything; they preserve the dream of a complete intelligibility of history. They do not resign themselves to being fragmentary mirrors, with only limited powers of comprehension. They consider still valid the pretention of Enlightenment man who, setting himself up as a mirror of the past, believed that he could read the movement towards the future – which is to say, that progress, with its consciousness of freedom, in which Hegel identified the onward march of History. In their irrational desire for rationality, they maintain this direction and cultivate the mirage of total transparency. It is just that, without the hope of another heaven, they peer into the darkness, investigate the meanderings of History, to seek the diabolical ways of the Evil that has yet to be defeated and expiated.

Enigmas and Misunderstandings

We often come across the term 'plot' being used as a synonym for a 'secret pact' or 'conspiracy'. Almost as if they were equivalents, because of the thread of secrecy that unites them and the machinations and intrigue behind them. The landscape is shaped by power struggles that take place in the shadows, shielded from prying eyes. But it is exactly by highlighting the differences between them, by looking at remote historical periods and different political orders, that we can better grasp the peculiarity of each term.

At the heart of the secret pact [in Italian, *congiura*] is the oath, the solemn agreement to discretion and loyalty, the bond that binds the protagonists, a small group of resolute individuals who are ready for anything. This is what is indicated by the Latin *coniurare*, being made up of the prefix *cum*, which refers to a pact, and the verb *iurare*, which, although coming from *ius*, *iuris*, does not imply a union in obedience to the law but, rather, refers to swearing a private oath. From Thucydides to Herodotus, from Plutarch to Tacitus, from Suetonius to Sallust, the secret pact boasts a long and ancient tradition, as attested by a vast literature. The Latin *coniuratio* is a calque of the Greek *sunomosía*. Nothing stirs greater fears in the city – not even revolt or civil war. For the secret pact immediately reveals its subversive potential. Beyond his plans themselves, the member of the pact compromises and oversteps – if only symbolically – the oath on which the *pólis* is based. The state of exception is already set in motion. A joint oath is sworn, creating an alternative bond, which mirrors the constituted authorities. Bound by the secret pact, by the utterance of words with a juridical-sacramental value, the members of the pact form a group of their own, a faction, a consortium.[1]

Over the centuries, the secret pact has retained the peculiar traits of a form of political struggle that, while justified by noble ideals, does not stop at using violence in its work of undermining power. Through daggers, poison, tyrannicide, the elimination of the powerful, the coup d'état, sedition, the restoration of legitimate government, the return to freedom is achieved. In participating in a ruthless and risky enterprise, the members of the clandestine pact know that they are sacrificing their lives. The recourse to a sacrificial, purifying and founding violence, capable of establishing another order, a new sovereignty, thus often finds legitimacy in a consecrated space and time. It is in the dark corridors of the royal palace, in the protected half-light of the church, that the assassins operate, most often during some liturgical celebration or festive occasion. Thus, in that sacred enclosure, the perpetrator exonerates himself and endows his nefarious act with a certain nobility. An extreme act of liberation, the secret pact can in turn become a festive occasion.

Perhaps more than anyone else, Machiavelli scrutinised, with depth and disenchantment, the innermost recesses of the secret pact, which in his thought became a political category. We need only recall the *Discourses on Livy*, of which a part (book III, chapter VI) was published in Paris in 1575 under the title *Traité des conjurations*. In the complex phenomenology that emerges from his writings, the secret pact is as dastardly and reckless as it is deserving of consideration, because it is a political act that, although often doomed to failure, can influence the balance of power. For Machiavelli, who was also personally involved – for example in an action against the Medici – the secret pact, a dramatic gesture that already dramatises politics, intensifies the conflict by calling the people itself onto the stage.

Indeed, the members of the secret pact end up coming out into the open: they have a name, a face, they are individuals in the flesh, protagonists of specific historical events. Equally concrete, represented by the figure of the prince or sovereign, is the power they aim at, which they want to overthrow, replace, conquer. It could be said that Machiavelli himself represents a watershed between the modern scenario of the secret pact and the more contemporary one of the plot – that is, between a physically identifiable power and a metaphysics of power. It is no coincidence that in the democratic context there is hardly any talk of secret pacts – solemn, grand, and increasingly consigned to the past.

The plot should also be distinguished from the conspiracy, although the influence of the English language leads even Italians to use these terms as equivalents. On the other hand, 'conspiracy' is a basis for indictment in several legal systems. Yet, even in this case, the differences ought not be overlooked. This is a vocabulary of political struggle, and its semantic field is articulated by the Latin. The word *conspiratio* comes from *cum* and *spirare*, which literally means to breathe together, in tune and in agreement. But here there is no oath, no sacred bond. It means whispering in secret to one's peer, murmuring to one's comrade, in hushed tones concerting some joint action against the established authorities, the state, the institutions. Held together by a common inspiration, the conspiracy can also become a revolt. Dictionaries and lexicons therefore emphasise its subversive notes.

Confirmation for this comes from the noun 'conspirator', synonymous with 'revolutionary'. The secrecy of his conduct is dictated by the repressive nature of power itself, which he cannot confront openly. Today's conspirator is tomorrow's insurgent. His actions are illegal, but not illegitimate. So, he expects the judgement of posterity. This nineteenth- and twentieth-century figure, of often legendary traits, has fuelled decades of literature and, indeed, has not been condemned by history. There is nothing abject, unworthy, or contemptible about being a conspirator. We need only think of the Carbonari, the members of the – mostly democratic – secret societies, who in Europe at least fought against monarchical regimes. One example especially worth mentioning is the Italian revolutionary Filippo Buonarroti, who later became a French citizen, a friend of Gracchus Babeuf, faithful to egalitarian-communist ideals, the tireless source of countless revolts, the emblem of the conspirator. To him we owe the famous 1828 work *History of Babeuf's Conspiracy for Equality*, in which, after Babeuf's death sentence, as he reconstructs the events of a revolt that was discovered and denounced in advance, he vindicates the word 'conspiracy'.[2]

Of course, there is nothing to deny the possibility that, in the half-light – where dreamers, revolutionaries, anarchists, and secret agents operate, in that 'world that never was', as Alex Butterworth called it in his fascinating book – boundaries will soften and roles will be reversed.[3]

But what, then, is a plot [*complotto*]? How should we define it? What concept goes together with it? Connoisseurs and aficionados of definitions will be disappointed. Even the attempt to grasp, once and for all, the essence of the 'plot', which eludes and dissimulates, is bound to remain unsatisfactory.[4] Perhaps etymology could come in useful here, as it does in other cases, But its origin hides more than one enigma. What is certain is that the word *complot* circulated in Old French, at the end of the twelfth century, with the sense of 'compact crowd'. So, in a now forgotten feminine form, it must have meant a gathering, an indistinct mass, an assemblage – like a line-up during battle. At the threshold of modernity, *complot* migrated from French into other languages: Italian, Spanish, German, Swedish, Portuguese, etc. And, in that transition, the more concrete meaning gradually gave way to the more abstract one of 'understanding common to several people'. From a huddled mass to an agreement, from indistinct union to an entente, from the cohesion of bodies to the union of minds.

Other clues are more ambiguous and uncertain. For example, the assonance with *comploit*, from the Latin *complex*, accomplice, or from *cum-plicare*, to envelop, to hold together. But there are also those who have seen in the Italian *complotto* the diminutive of *comble* – full, crammed – from the Latin *cumulus*, which means not only accumulation but also a pile or an aggregation of people. Some etymologists have even gone so far as to imagine a verb *com-peloter*: on this reading, it derives from game known as *pelota*, so-called because of the ball formed by tightly woven strings of rope covered by a casing. Several traits of the plot, from the inextricability of the strings to the outer covering, recur in this fanciful version, though there is a lack of proof for such a reading.

Far more reliable and interesting is its etymological path in English, in which *complot* immediately comes upon the verb 'to plot' – to outline a plan, to draw a diagram. The overlapping and synergy between the two terms can then easily be identified: 'plot' would increasingly come to mean a union in view of some design or scheme. Better, it means this secret plan, this machination, itself. The figurative value comes to dominate, especially given that 'plot' also means the weaving of the web, the pattern of a tale. From its original military surroundings, 'plot' transitioned to the narrative context, where it sank lasting roots, albeit without ever losing its political meaning.

If in the secret pact there are faces and names, indeed ones which have often gone down in history, the plot is a compact and indistinct mass, a collective whose individuals remain unknown, a nameless whole, a faceless conglomerate. The plot is a vague and nebulous entity, opaque and elusive. There is no oath, no solemn promise,

not even a common inspiration or aspiration. Nothing
that looks like an explicit agreement. Only a dark tangle,
a dense muddle, in which barely the trace of a pattern can
be made out. Mystery hovers over this web of ties; it is per-
meated and held together by enigma. This superior, hidden
'understanding' is so lacking in personality as to suggest
that some uncanny autonomous mechanism is at work.

Here, then, is the Plot, or, rather, Power. This is in fact
how power is imagined in the contemporary world, faceless and nameless, the power that always and everywhere
dominates, that cannot be grasped in any place or moment
– the network of automatic commands, the occult, hierar-
chical prism, the techno-media operation that governs on
a planetary scale.

For people stripped of the subversive force they once
had, confused and disoriented by the darkness and fog,
the plot appears on the other side of the barricade. They
no longer conspire, they no longer take aim at the established authorities. For those who might sense that a plot is
afoot – in English, commonly called 'conspiracists', not-
withstanding the etymological distinctions we have just
made – fighting against the 'hidden power' wielded by the
sophisticated coordinators or lowly agents means unmasking it, searching against the odds to put a face and a name
on the intrigue. All this also has an effect on the term 'plot'
itself, intensifying and expanding its meaning. It adds on a
surplus: the plot becomes global and everlasting.

Even more misleading is the phrase 'conspiracy theories', which has also been in vogue in Italian for a couple
of decades now, a source of numerous misunderstandings.
'Teorie del complotto' appears in Italian as a translation of the English 'conspiracy theories', introduced by
Karl Popper in his 1945 book *The Open Society and its
Enemies*, but attested by the Oxford Dictionary in 1909
and probably in circulation already in the nineteenth
century. It almost goes without saying that here the term
'theory' – far from pointing to the rigour and seriousness
of scientific method – has a pejorative sense, referring to

a fantastical hypothesis, a mere rumour, a superstitious belief, a groundless pseudo-explanation. But this not only gives this term a censorious note – prey as it is to a superficial and illusory 'anti-conspiracism' – but it commits the serious strategic error of reducing 'conspiracy theories' to criteria of true and false. This not only bypasses the real problem but heads into a blind alley. The effects of this quest to find objective criteria of filtering and evaluation are only harmful. For the sense that a plot is afoot cannot be measured or judged – or dismissed. It is not reducible to theoretical hypotheses, and for this reason it escapes any dichotomy of truth and falsehood. Moreover, for those who believe in the plot, the absence of evidence is itself the most damning proof. What some take for conspiratorial fantasies may, for others, be the workings of a very real plot.

If anything, it would be more accurate to speak of 'narratives revolving around plots' – a phrase which better grasps certain characteristics of this phenomenon, somewhere in between history writing and fictional readings. So, we need to abandon this whole craze for definitions and approach this phenomenon in its current, complex dimensions.

The Workings of the Plot

The plot is usually seen from the outside and in an instrumental way. Somewhere, a plot is in the works. Or it has already occurred and may repeat itself. It is thus conceived – depending on one's evaluation – as a superstition, a pathology, a menace, a poison.

Perhaps, ultimately, a change of perspective is needed, to consider the plot from the inside. Then, the plot becomes more extensive, graver still. What thus appears, above all, is the political form that is left over, in the age of the eclipse of politics. It is not just any form but an 'apparatus' [*Gestell*] in the sense in which philosophy has developed this concept in its reflections on technology. The plot is not merely one among the various instruments that power makes use of. Rather, it is the apparatus in which power is articulated, exercised, dissimulated. It is the mask of power in the time of a faceless power.

Precisely because it is a double-faced intrigue, the plot responds to the splitting of reality characteristic of contemporary politics in its profound metaphysics. Never before has reality seemed so tightly programmed and planned, to the point of being wholly predictable. Never before has it proven so fragile and insubstantial, to the point of stirring an unprecedented disquiet.

Since the word has never lost its metaphorical value, when someone speaks of a 'plot' we imagine a pattern, a web of ties, a warp that can expand. What is certain is that this image has itself expanded and the plot has become as vast as the world. Technology has decisively contributed to this. The web has connected the world, linked it from pole to pole, surrounded and circumscribed it, to the point of altering its very image. The world of the web is the technical representation of the world: telematic cables, power lines, synthetic fibres, moving streams that, in a maze of nodes, a labyrinth of connections, run, branch, intersect in the air, in the depths of the oceans, in the meanders of the earth. Hard and soft technology take turns across the longitudes and latitudes of cyberspace. They do not merely inform – they form. They order, set up, regulate.

We are no longer beads in God's abacus. We are caught in the omnipresent web that secretly arranges the world. Invisible lines and impalpable cables follow us everywhere. Where messages are arriving and departing, power manifests itself and suspicion mounts. Suddenly, the world appears to be organised and controlled by an enormous plot. The world has become a plot – the plot has become the world. But the reference to the image ought not lead us astray: this is not just a question of spatiality and visibility. The plot is the form in which we now understand the world and inhabit it.

When we speak of an 'apparatus', we mean this as a translation of the famous term *Gestell* that Martin Heidegger introduced into philosophy, in reference to the apparatus of technology.[1] Set up for the purposes of domination and control – but as if it were a neutral instrument in service of a liberated humanity – technology reveals its dark, disturbing face. For some time now, the mechanism has run out of control; its gears turn autonomously, the apparatus orders and arranges. The modern subject is convinced that he can dominate everything through technology – yet this subjectivity is itself undermined. The designer becomes the designed. And he discovers that he is employed in an unlimited production, left as a mere official in the order-producing factory.

The world of the plot is the one governed and oriented by the apparatus of technology, where reality is constructed, if not manipulated, by the media web. But the 'apparatus', in Giorgio Agamben's reading of Michel Foucault's thought, also refers to the *oikonomia* – that is, the governmental machine, the pure and simple administration proper to the era in which politics is suspended.[2] This incessantly turning machine, instead of following a providential plan of salvation, risks leading the world towards catastrophe.

We cannot grasp the vast dimensions of the plot, which has taken on truly planetary proportions, if we do not understand that it is more than a matter of technology and also see its economic and political aspect. The plot is, in fact, the constitutive form of a world made to submit to capitalist *hubris* and dominated by the omnipotence of the state. The state – this artificial and deeply ambiguous construct, the promise of protection and security, the threat of capture and insecurity – is itself the great spectre of the plot. This is no longer just a matter of grey bureaucratic apparatuses, the secret services, the quintessential example of espionage and covert activity. Rather, the state itself, in its close connection to technology and capitalism, increasingly appears as one vast plot. In essence, this is the most recent and striking revelation, which the totalitarian calling of the plot had already foreshadowed. For some time now, the political landscape has been alarmed by the ghost of the world-state, a source of apprehension and subject of accusations. The state plot thus itself becomes not just far-reaching, but global.

How to escape all this? Where is there to flee to? There are no easy ways out. Under the Empire of the Plot, each and every person is left defenceless in the face of an inscrutable techno-state apparatus. The faceless power is secretly disseminated with a cunning opacity that makes it impossible to detect its traces, to follow its threads. Each and every person is thrown into the vertigo of the plot, where they sense that they are being manoeuvred by unknown hands, who are in turn manoeuvred. So, their existence is both hyper-organised and completely unpredictable. If the plot is at the heart of the state, this is because power is exercised not only *by means of the plot*. For it also functions *thanks to the threat* of other plots, coming from the enemy within or other external enemies, constantly evoked as a warning and a challenge to survival itself.

Is it possible to deconstruct the metaphysics of politics, without waiting for the always elusive revelation of the secret? If it is not possible, then everything will instead rely on the spasmodic and inconclusive wait for the plot to be unmasked and the double reality to be broken apart. Only then would the seeming but fictitious reality coincide with the hidden but true reality. But is there really a secret, a final knowledge, an ultimate foundation on which everything stands? Or is the secret precisely the non-existence of the secret, of any ultimate foundation? To claim access to another reality, a hidden and true one, beyond the visible one would be lethal and self-destructive.

This is what becomes clear from George Orwell's *1984*, where State and Plot interpenetrate in a biopolitical order that intervenes in even the most intimate corners of human life. As in a long journey of initiation, the ultimate secret is the non-existence of the secret: at the base of this order there is not an ultimate knowledge or an ultimate foundation. *Not* putting faith in such a knowledge, *not* looking for it, is the way to salvation, the possibility of survival.

The plot must, then, be unmasked – but only if it is understood as that apparatus of power that represents an archaic necessity, because it makes us believe that we can and must seek an *arché*, a principle and a command in the explanation of the world and its events.

Democracy and Power

If conspiracism were a mere residue of the past, it would surely go ever more out of fashion. But the opposite is true – it is so widespread in today's democracies that it seems to be a far from trivial aspect of them. But why? How can we explain the surprising – yet so intimate – link between the plot and democracy? Only the key word 'power' can offer the answer.

To grasp this, it is enough to cast a brief glance at the beginning of democratic modernity. It was in the new political landscape produced by the French Revolution that the plot took root and gained strength. Only by observing it in that context can we grasp its present meaning.

For those alive today, inheritors to a centuries-old legacy, it is difficult even vaguely to imagine the great surprise that was the Revolution of 1789. Never before had there been such an exceptional, vast, devastating – and thus also indecipherable and arcane – event. This oldest of European monarchies had been swept away abruptly, but the deeper upheaval had shattered the old order forever. The gates of history had finally opened to the multitude, coming out into the open to become the protagonists of their own lives. Politics was reaching the masses and the masses took the floor in the public arena. Here was the sovereign people, here was democracy.

Who could have concocted such a diabolical action – a wicked, subversive plot against monarchy, the established powers, private property, and the Christian faith? This gave rise to the conspiracist vision of the French Revolution, which heralded the long line of interpretations aimed at eliminating any element of chance from historical explanation: if something happened, it was because someone wanted it to. Following in the footsteps of Augustin Barruel, who had provided the canonical reading in his *Memoirs to Serve the History of Jacobinism* in 1797–8, many counter-revolutionaries angrily alleged a Jacobin–Masonic plot concocted by the *philosophes*, the exponents of the Enlightenment.

But this flair for identifying plots was also at work on the other side of the barricades. From the outset, the revolutionaries denounced treacherous plots and the secret activities of monarchists, clerics and foreign agents that threatened the *Patrie* and freedom. An accusing finger was pointed at the plots by aristocrats. As suspicion began to mount everywhere, figures from Saint-Just to Marat called for pre-emptive measures. Robespierre was the champion of vigilance against a shadowy, relentless plot. With the increasingly Manichaean perspective of a division between patriots and the guilty, the plunge into the Terror loomed.

In his book on the French Revolution, the historian François Furet emphasised the importance that the idea of the plot took on. It seems almost cut from the same cloth as revolutionary consciousness itself.[1] It is as if the search for occult power plagued democracy from the start.

The people was finally sovereign. But where was power now to be found? When power had been concentrated in the body of the king, it could easily be identified. But with the destruction of the royalist order and the advent of democracy, it was hard to tell where it had gone. It seemed volatile, elusive. Power would now be entrusted, from one election to the next, to voting by citizens. Meaning, the people was the power. But speech alone guaranteed that power belongs to the people, that no one could appropriate it for themselves. The power of the people was in fact the power of no one. This produced an unprecedented vacuum: it would be filled only temporarily by speech, which is common and public, while power builds up its forces in secret.

Did power really end up in a vacuum? All that effort, just to arrive at such a disconcerting outcome? It is hard to believe that democracy is fully there: for the absolute foundation of the sovereign is supplanted by the absence of any foundation, any absolute. One can understand the amazement of citizens who found themselves cast into the landscape of democratic modernity. Along with this astonishment, there was also uncertainty, perplexity, anxiety. The power of the people is an enigma, a mysterious 'void' that, on closer inspection, soon fills up with spectres. These are the spectres of the plot: hidden behind the appearance of the newly conquered power is the real power of occult forces. This imaginary supplants the idea of the sovereign. This is the same metaphysics that favours the idea that a plot is afoot; for it makes it impossible to get rid of the myth of power.

On the other hand, the anxious search to demystify an invisible power remains a dark evil, gnawing away at contemporary democracy from within. Indeed, it represents a grave danger to democracy. Undoubtedly, power today appears increasingly elusive, ubiquitous, and web-like. Projected through the channels of technology and the flows of the economy, it lacks any centre and perhaps any direction. It has no face, no name, no address. The unease felt by those under the sway of power lies in their inability to locate where it is. They perceive only the diffuse presence of power, which adds to their uncertainty and suspicion. Effect leads back to cause. Scepticism turns into the dogmatic certainty that there must be some hidden locus of power. Thus emerge the dark spectres of the plot, which haunt the political scene. They grow ever greater in number when the king has no clothes, when the power ruling the planetary economy cannot avoid coming out into the open.

The current crisis of politics stems largely from this question – 'where is power?' Yet the question is also a misleading one. As Claude Lefort and Michel Foucault suggested, in two perspectives that mirror one another, seeking to locate power is a futile endeavour. On closer inspection, it is both everywhere and nowhere, because it inhabits a different place in each instance and operates differently in each of them.[2]

Rather, the spasmodic search for 'occult forces' only expresses the profound inability to live a democratic life. Democracy is always riven with permanent dissent, agitated by a disconcertion which can never be overcome. In a now famous line, Lefort saw democracy's revolutionary trait in the 'locus of power that becomes an *empty place*'.[3] The absence of a foundation, the division, the openness: in the democratic community, the people can proclaim itself sovereign only in a symbolic sense and never in a substantive and identifiable one. The people cannot occupy the place of power, which must instead remain empty.

Those who do want to fill this space set out to close the community body in on itself, abolishing any otherness. This otherness is itself projected outwards – perhaps in the image of a foreigner, an enemy. This was Donald Trump's political strategy, aimed at disqualifying and delegitimising democracy. The spectre of the plot then risks slipping into the phantoms of totalitarianism. Governing by evoking the nightmare of chaos, the bogeyman of the 'Deep State' and the occult global government is a caricatural – yet fearsome – way to ride the wave of discontent, directing it not within the democratic framework but against it.

Deformed by the conspiracist reading, impatience, frustration, and *ressentiment* can instil that 'hatred of democracy' highlighted by Jacques Rancière.[4] In the systematic denunciation of the 'real powers-that-be' which snatch away the people's sovereignty by ruling for their own profit, the politics of conspiracism in many ways converges with populism. In each case, a secret machination is held to blame for the gap between the idea of democracy and its realisation.

The Cause of All Our Ills

If global crisis is mounting, if events keep going downhill, someone somewhere will have to answer for it. An explanation must be found for the seemingly inexplicable. A banking collapse, a judicial scandal, a political assassination must be traced back to 'the guilty'. To a name, a place, a face. In its 'alternative' interpretation, conspiracism reproduces itself, reiterates the same causal pattern. What has happened is the effect of some cause that needs discovering. More than that: what happened is the outcome of the intentions of a subject – be it individual or collective – that acted in its own, usually well-disguised, interests.

So, eyes are opened and ears pricked to make out the evidence, collect the clues, decipher the signs, before the conclusion can thus be deduced. The conspiracist plays the role of the diagnostician, in between that of psychoanalyst and investigator. The causal explanation seems, first and foremost, to fill a cognitive void, the need to know. But it is not difficult to discern other aims behind this one. The search for the cause is, at the same time, also the indictment. This indictment implicitly contains a moral condemnation. But uncovering a plot means not only denouncing the guilty party but also stigmatising him as a political enemy, often even demonising him. The denunciation is already a raising-of-the-drawbridge, the beginning of a witch-hunt, if not a call to arms or even a licence for extermination.[1]

The landscape is brimming with occult powers, nefarious manipulators, satanic figures, all of them so many sources of evil. It is necessary constantly to watch out for them – and ceaselessly to uncover their hidden agendas. It was in this regard that Léon Poliakov, the great historian of antisemitism, introduced the effective formula 'diabolical causality' to refer to the relentless search for perfidious and abject agents who could be blamed for the world's ills. The Jews, for instance. In his preface to his 1980 work *La causalité diabolique: essai sur l'origine des persécutions*, Poliakov acknowledged his debt to an enlightening observation by Albert Einstein, who had, already in 1927, warned against the belief in demonic actors at the root of the concept of causality.[2] Einstein had recently read Lucien Lévy-Bruhl's essay on the primitive mentality. But it is interesting that Poliakov – as he himself admits – arrived at this formula by studying the totalitarian phenomena of the twentieth century. Underlying them was the belief that the real movements of political life are manoeuvred by hidden causes, operating behind the scenes. The worst happens when, as in the case of Hitler, the champions of conspiratorial thinking rise to power. In Hitler's demonology, the Jews were the forces of Evil, the eschatological enemies.

But we can go further than Poliakov and say that Nazism embodied the archaic passion for the ultimate cause, the regression towards the causal power of an Other who is pulling the strings of chaos and destruction. At the heart of the Shoah was the human difficulty of dealing with existential angst and political instability.

Such a 'police conception of history' was, Manès Sperber suggested, unconfessed and yet widely practised, even after Nazism, in more or less democratic regimes.[3] The idea that we can reach salvation once the cause of all evils has been ascertained (and eliminated) is thus well established.

The more devastating and shocking the effects, the more powerful and frightening the causes must be – the Jews, Capital, the CIA, Bill Gates. Conspiratorial thinking takes proportions into account. It works by re-establishing a sort of explanatory order, which traces the march of events back to the malevolent agendas of subjects who consciously work up plans and develop ever-well-concealed designs. Almost any text on 'conspiracy theories' is bound to cite Popper, who already in his 1945 book *The Open Society and its Enemies*, and later also in *Conjectures and Refutations*, emphasises the connection with the framework of chance. Those who look for plots are driven by a form of belief, or rather superstition, which prompts them not only to look for culprits but also to believe that everything desirable is also achievable. Chance is obliterated, all unknowns eliminated; it is as if everything really always happens in preordained fashion. This is why 'the conspiracy theory of society' is, in Popper's view, as primitive as theism: the gods, whose whims and wills governed the fate of mankind for the ancients, have been superseded by sinister groups or suspicious individuals, on whose demonic interventions any misfortune can be blamed.[4]

There thus took root a widespread way of understanding conspiracism as a reaction to the 'disenchantment of the world', as per Max Weber's famous interpretative model. That is, magical thinking survived despite – or, better, in antithesis to – growing rationalisation. It is thus presented as a deeply anti-modern phenomenon, an irrational return to the past by those who prefer to close their eyes and not accept 'more self-evident' and more uncomfortable 'explanations'. This peremptory judgement, in condemnation of such thinking, would be taken up and successfully re-elaborated by Umberto Eco.

Yet, on closer inspection, already before this Friedrich Nietzsche had subjected the causal system to a sharp criticism, which would leave it indelibly marked. '*We* are the ones who invented causation ... and if we project and inscribe this symbol world onto things as an "in-itself", then this is the way we have always done things, namely *mythologically*.'[5] The need to assign a cause betrays an irrepressible need for security, the intolerability of all that is new, unknown, enigmatic. It thus reveals apprehension, fear, weakness. Causality is not a theoretical schema, but an impulse. Nietzsche mounts a merciless diagnosis: 'The causal drive is therefore determined and stimulated by the feeling of fear.'[6] The psychological need to believe in a cause resides in the impossibility – human, all too human – of imagining an event with no intentionality behind it. This is why, according to Nietzsche, attributing a cause and attributing an intention amount to the same act. We take everything that happens for an action that therefore presupposes an agent, a subject endowed with will – i.e. the power to produce effects. In so doing, we humanise the world in our own image and then assume that this interpretation is an objective structure. We do not admit that reality is processual and phenomena are complex. Even if this is just our own ingenious representation, we prefer to live in a world of mirages and the will o' the wisp in order to be able to explain things – i.e. to make the unusual fit in with the usual and shake off the disturbing impression of the alien and strange. So, to know is not to explore the unknown but, rather, to reduce it to the known. We have absolutely no interest in getting to know but simply wish not to be shaken in our imperturbable faith that we already know. Any explanation is preferable to the lack of one.

This is not simply a question of a primitive mentality or an irrational view, as Popper, among others, argues. The question runs rather deeper. Following Nietzsche, demonic causality can be said to be a metaphysical passion. We look for the cause – that is, identify the culprit behind the scenes, that evil agent, endowed with the sovereign power to harm, that unique and absolute enemy hiding in the dark netherworld. In the Manichaean opposition of light and darkness, good and evil, that characterises the metaphysical, the absolute enemy embodies the dark Evil. Everything is permitted, in the name of self-defence against this destructive agent. Evil comes from the outside – from elsewhere, from the netherworld where the satanic enemy lurks, causing tragic and devastating events.

From this perspective, conspiracism is merely the heightened version of a metaphysical politics.

Hungry for Myths

The imagination is not usually recognised as having a role in the political context, which is instead taken for the domain of rational criteria and values. All that does not fit into stringent argument by reason, all that springs from the most arcane recesses of oneiric vastness, is relegated to a shadow zone that thus seems impenetrable. Dream, myth, and utopia were banished from the public space already decades ago. This is the result not only of capitalist hyper-realism passing off every alternative as totalitarian but also of the rationalisation of life by technology.

Yet who could convincingly argue that dreams play no part in the twists and turns of politics? Even a look at the most recent past shows that the great upheavals of the last few centuries have been promoted and accompanied – for better or worse – by a powerful imagination. We could cite many such examples. What would have become of Marxism if, reduced to a dialectical-scientific system, it had lacked its prophetic appeal and its charge of messianism? But similar considerations could also be made for all manner of millenarianism, backward-looking nostalgia, personality cults, harmful obsessions, and plots. Moreover, we can see that all this has also left its footprints on the current political landscape.

We should rightly speak of this imaginary in terms of 'myth'. There are different interpretations of this term, which can be judged even in opposite ways: for some, it is a smokescreen, a mystification that distorts the truth of facts and contravenes the rules of logic, while, for others, it is a tale that, while proceeding from the past, retains a certain explanatory power in the present and the future. Beginning with Nietzsche and Freud, in the twentieth century myth came back in vogue. Like dreams, myth escapes all conceptual reduction, and it fuses together contents from different eras. What especially stands out is the cyclical temporality of myth, which, despite the brakes of Enlightenment reason, has forcefully re-emerged each time it has appeared to be destroyed. Not by chance, Carl Gustav Jung understood it as an archetype of the collective unconscious that remains alive in the depths of peoples, like a narrative casing which survives every moment of rupture without ever falling apart. There is a short step from here to mass ideologies.

Mircea Eliade famously said that 'the myth relates a sacred history, that is, a primordial event that took place at the beginning of time, ab initio.'[1] In addition to being a legendary tale, myth offers an interpretative grid, a set of hermeneutic keys that can help restore order to the bewildering chaos of events into which the world seems to be plunging. It thus has its own associative syntax, its own intimate logic, a code in which it transcribes its message and through which that message is then to be understood and deciphered, its own labyrinthine coherence that also represents the promise of a guiding thread. In this sense it has its own absolute truth, able to withstand anything that may belie it.

It would also be reductive not to see its mobilising potential. Indeed, this becomes clear in the case of political myths, a contemporary version of the great sacred myths.

Fluid and ambivalent as necessary to attach itself, with its own flexible framework, to new realities, the political myth has a disruptive force that it would be wrong to underestimate. It was Georges Sorel who highlighted its explosive energy, with particular reference to the general strike, the myth par excellence of the proletariat, 'in which Socialism is wholly comprised'.[2]

The political myths of the present are what has been left over in the political imaginary after the end of grand narratives. It is surely true that the general strike does not today bear the mythical appeal it did in times past. However, the myths that do still exist are all the more pervasive. The plot occupies a special place among them. It is a myth from the most distant past which survives in a posthumous existence like no other. This should give pause for thought about the present era, if the myth of the plot not only refers to the occult site of power but, moreover, levels an accusation and, at the same time, raises the alarm for self-defence.

To understand how this imaginary can still exert a hold today, it is worth drawing on a formula – if not always a transparent one – used by Furio Jesi: the 'mythological machine'.[3] Myth is the sacred story, which attempts to fill the primordial distance that stands as an abyss between men and gods, as in the Greek landscape, where it was called *chàos*. But Greek mythology is not inextricably bound to the fate of the Greek gods; it has been preserved even after the gods have fled and the 'death of God' has been proclaimed. Even those who are not persuaded of this are themselves part of that mourning. The 'mythological machine' is a contraption that fuses various mythological materials – opaque images, enigmatic cults, magic formulas, arcane symbols, occult rituals – combining past and present, or, rather, myth and history. This is mystification not because it connects different epochs and cultures but, rather, because it provides a homogeneous view of historical time and above all alludes to a secret source, beyond history, an eternal present of the myth.

Making things more explicit, we could speak of archaic depths, an archic foundation. The mythological machine is, in fact, self-founding, in the sense that it places its own origin outside and beyond itself, in a remote source which usually remains intangible. Instead, as in a shop that stocks junk, knick-knacks, and bric-à-brac, the machine puts together the materials of mythology, taking them here and there, trying to breathe new life into them. Its recipe consists of sprinkling these happily inert materials with the colour of life, in order to make them easily palatable. For example, hooked crosses, runic symbols, and fasces. The result is a dark and kitschy product. Those who consume it experience the fatuous intoxication of contact with that mythical and secret source, which is otherwise denied them. This temporarily quells their hunger for myths, though it always remains unsatisfied. Theodore Ziolkowski referred to this to point to the striking tendency towards the 'gastronomy of the soul' in 1920s Germany, thereby indicating the human condition which is both presupposed and fomented by the mythological machine.[4]

Those who hunger for myths, in the absence of the original, instead make do with mythological sustenance. The junk they feed on is far from harmless; indeed, it is literally lethal, because it carries the threat of death and can lead to death. This morphological skeleton, this pattern of stereotypes, formulas, symbols, and rituals, almost always finds a cynical political use for maintaining order.

Can we simply call this 'right-wing culture'? Evidently not. It would be better to frame the mythological machine within a broader, nostalgic, and backward-looking culture, which is deeply reactionary because it reacts not only to the unknown of the present but also to the shortage of the means of interpretation that help read the world. Unable to work out new coordinates, this culture is content with old leftovers. Such a judgement can also apply to the left.

So, the myth of the plot, which survives so pervasively, is not really a myth at all but actually the outcome of the mythological machine – or, rather, apparatus. The web stretched over the world, enveloping and engulfing it, does not only have the metallic sterility of technology. For it is also enlivened by the dead flesh of mythology. This alchemy is what makes it so serious – so deadly.

The Prague Cemetery:
The Backdrop to the Plot

Somewhere there is the gathering place of those who pull the strings, who weave the plot. Access to that place, difficult and risky, is an initiatory passage, a descent into the darkness, penetrating into the dungeons of power. The threshold metaphysically separates good and evil, light and darkness, day and night, freedom and despotism, justice and arbitrariness, transparency and mystery, life and death. Conceived as an inverted pyramid, the image of the plot represents, in perhaps the most intense and most straightforward way, the antithesis of the universal order.

Whether it is a hidden chamber, a lodge's underground hideout, a basement, a crypt, or even a cemetery, the site of the plot – protected by a banal and misleading exterior or by a forbidding entrance – is the bloodless heart of the deadly machinery, the gloomy seat of domination, the spectral *arché* of the apparatus. The political architecture is reiterated in the symbolism that is thus transmitted: distant yet close, peripheral yet central, that impenetrable site, within the community's own inner space, is the place of sovereign exception. There, the laws, indeed, all the rules of normality, are evaded. The adepts of the plot,

strangers coming from elsewhere, foreigners who have
a secret code and evil customs, indulge only their own
appetites and obey their own imperatives. They prefer the
night, when the shadows thicken, when no one is identifiable, when all light of familiarity is extinguished. Gloomy
and glacial, wrapped in dark clothes or white shrouds,
they are disturbing spectres emerging from the catacomb
underground, rising from beyond the grave to stand as
overseers and judges, capable of animating automatons
and draining all lifeblood.

The backdrop to the plot, where the final threads of
intrigue are knotted, has certain constant traits. The iconography is rich and there is an extraordinary narrative
variety – but they follow the same score, reworking a single
outline. The plot essentially conceals the same pattern. In
the immense literature on this subject, three tales appear
emblematic not only because of their similar structure, sen-
sationalist style, and depth of imagery but also because of
their mythological value in the political imaginary. These
are tales of three plots: the Jewish, Jesuitical, and Masonic.
Comparing them, we find a pattern destined to repeat
itself. If the Jesuitical theme would become exhausted, the
other two would converge in the archetype of all plots: the
'Jewish-Masonic' one.[1]

The first story is from the pen of Hermann O. F. Gödsche,
a former official in the Prussian Post Office who, under
the pseudonym Sir John Retcliffe, published the medio-
cre novel *Biarritz* in 1868, including a chapter entitled
'The rabbi's speech'. The fantastical tale soon passed for
a forged 'document'. This was not yet the *Protocols of
the Elders of Zion*, though thanks to Gödsche it now had
its literary model. It was thanks to a plot – a convoluted
detective story – that the myth of the Jewish plot could be
created just a few years later. This myth does not have a
beginning, since the original does not exist. But nor does
it have an end – for, even though this myth led to extermination, it remains the fulcrum of recurrent antisemitic
mobilisations.[2]

In Prague's old ghetto, where Jews lived for centuries com-
pletely apart, a peculiar ring of crumbling houses, backing
on to each other, surrounds and closes, as if to protect it, a
high wall, in places eroded and crumbling. The wild shrubs
and elder branches may give a misleading impression.
Behind that wall does not breathe a gust of melancholic
peace, as would befit a resting place but, rather, the spirit
of a people who, condemned to eternal wandering after suf-
fering, struggle and persecution, have not found peace there
either. It is as if the graves, which confusedly overlap, one
layer after another, for lack of soil, bent by the wind and
covered with undergrowth, suddenly opened up, allowing
the sandstone tombstones to rise from the deep undersoil.
The oldest known Jewish cemetery, this city of the dead is
called the 'abode of life', as if a mysterious impulse could be
born from there, overturning the fates, making the exiles of
times past the new masters of the world. It would seem the
planetary sovereignty to come is hidden in the dark depths
of that desert of tombs. Among the gravestones stands out,
not by chance, that of Rabbi Löw, the Maharal of Prague,
the great kabbalist, the one who defeated death by mag-
ically giving life to the Golem, the clay machine able to
avenge the Jewish people.

Two men have arranged to meet at night: the first, tall and
with unmistakable Germanic features, has a spiritual and
strong-willed appearance; the other also betrays his origin,
through his pallor and facial features. They are a young
scholar from Berlin, able to decipher ancient languages, to
understand even Caldaic, and an Italian Jew who has had
some baptismal water poured over his head – a Marrano,
in short – whose name Lasali evokes that of the famous
socialist. They are bound together by a pact made three
years earlier in the catacombs of Rome, when the Italian
Jew, bragging of his doctrine and knowledge, had promised
the other, out of gratitude for saving him from danger, to
reveal to him the secrets of the Kabbalah, Jewish mysticism,
the key to every plot against the whole world. Aware of the
mortal risks, the two of them head out through the winding
alleys of the Prague ghetto and, through a narrow opening,
penetrate into the cemetery where, in a dark corner, they
wait with bated breath.

At eleven o'clock, when the clocktower has just tolled its chimes, the gates of the cemetery creak ajar. Confused shadows, wrapped in long white tallit *shawls, slip stealthily into the freezing night. One after the other, they kneel before a gravestone, touching it with their foreheads three times as they whisper a prayer. The scene is repeated each time for the exponents of the twelve tribes of Israel. Midnight strikes when the thirteenth figure, representing the tribe of the exiles, kneels in front of a gravestone, takes his place alongside the others. This is the* sanhedrin *where, according to a millennia-old custom, every hundred years the tribes gather around the tomb of Master Caleb, the great Rabbi Simeon ben-Jehuda, to concert the plan for world conquest. A metallic sound rises from the grave and a blue flame casts a livid glow over the assembled. 'If eighteen centuries have belonged to our enemies, the present century and those to come must belong to us,' the rabbi proclaims, in the night of the Prague cemetery.*

Aaron, leader of the Levites, presides over proceedings. For each tribe there resounds the name of a European metropolis – Paris, London, Vienna, Amsterdam – as a sign of Jewish power, facilitated by progress. Each presents the balance sheet of recent years and proposes some machination: trafficking on the stock markets, pushing nations into debt, buying up land, the reduction of artisans to labourers, the destruction of churches, the undermining of armies, driving revolution, monopolising trade, taking over public functions, hegemonising culture, promoting mixed marriages, and subverting morals. Finally, Manasseh intervenes to say that none of this would be of any use if it were not thanks to the press, which turns injustice into justice, humiliation into honour, which separates families and shakes thrones. Aaron concludes by recalling that 'the whole earth shall belong to the people of Abraham, scattered over the earth.' The hour has never been closer. For gold is world domination: that is the secret of the Kabbalah. After Israel's millennia-long struggle, finally the new century will be the age of worldwide domination, the product of all manner of catastrophes. The gloomy night is pierced by the last flicker of the blue flame. Thus ends the meeting. But none of the participants have noticed the presence of the two men, the erudite German and the converted Italian Jew. Unseen, they finally swear to devote all their strength to fight that diabolical Jewish plot.

The second story is taken from Eugène Sue's *The Wandering Jew*, a novel that, published in serial form on the eve of 1848, added to the genre of anti-clerical polemics. The occult power denounced in its pages is that of the Society of Jesus, able to influence government decisions, play with the property of millions of people, and influence the course of history.

A grey October morning in 1831. At the end of a lonely street in Paris, one can just about make out a modest dwelling. Wedged into its drab façade are an arched doorway and two windows protected by thick iron bars. The interior is shrouded in silence. The walls of the large hall on the ground floor are panelled with grey wood; the red-tile floor has been meticulously polished. The windows are draped in white calico curtains. Standing at one end of the room, in front of the fireplace, is a sphere about four feet in diameter, set on a sturdy oak pedestal. Across this large globe is scattered a multitude of small red crosses: from north to south, from east to west, from the most barbaric countries and the most remote islands to the most civilised nations, all the way to France. There is no corner of the globe not coloured by these small crosses, evidently used as markers of control. In front of a black table, full of papers, bustles Mr Rodin, a man already of advanced years, dressed in a threadbare grey-green frock coat; his gaunt face, pointed chin and bloodless complexion suggest a livid mask, whose appearance seems all the stranger because of his sepulchral immobility, almost making him resemble a corpse. Using a cipher, he compiles coded messages. Everything in this leaden hall has a sinister aspect. The door knocker bangs, hollowly. At the entrance is a 35-year-old man with a haughty look and an authoritarian manner; his gestures exude energy and boldness. But, barely concealed, behind his powers of seduction, is the web of chicanery. His secretary Rodin is caught under his thumb. Laconic and impassive, he shows him a voluminous bundle of messages from the four corners of the Earth. And,

as he writes, the master paces back and forth until, con-
templating with a flicker of pride the immense web of red
crosses around the globe, he imperiously rests his vigorous
hand, betraying the certitude of his dominance.

The protagonist of the third tale is Cagliostro. His adven-
turous life inspires the novel *Joseph Balsamo*, published in
serial form between 1846 and 1849. Alexandre Dumas
gives fictional expression to the thesis earlier introduced
by Augustin Barruel, indeed one widespread at the time,
according to which the hurricane of revolution owed to
some prior conspiracy.

Evening thickens its shadow on the massifs lining the left
bank of the River Rhine. A path twists its way up the dark
slope and, as if crossing an impenetrable wall, is lost behind
the thick fir trees. The gloomy landscape is enough to make
one shiver. It is 6 May 1770. As the sun sets, a traveller
heads into the dense forest. Leaving his horse behind, he
sets off towards the dark interior. The only thing to guide
him is the mysterious glow of a lamp. When he reaches a
castle in ruins, he discovers that the light is emanating from
a ghostly figure, a phantom who, at the threshold of a circu-
lar room carpeted in black, invites him to enter. The tombs
burst open and a multitude of masked men take their place
on the steps of the room. The traveller – a foreigner, Italian
and perhaps Sicilian – does not appear intimidated and,
on the contrary, willingly submits to the cruel trials. He is
not afraid, because they do not know who he is, while he
already knows all their mysteries. Suddenly, he reveals: 'ego
sum qui sum.' He is the one they had been waiting for, the
one destined to unleash the salutary fire that will light up
the world. The torch is to be given to France, the vanguard
among nations. A fearful king, a corrupt throne – once this
keystone has been taken away, the entire monarchical edifice
will collapse, and the sovereigns of Europe will plunge into
the abyss. This will hasten the end of the old order and the
advent of the reign of Liberty and Equality. Around him,
the men of the subterranean crypts, representing the entire
Western world, applaud the systematic plan for subversion.

Philosophers, economists, and ideologues will shout at the top of their lungs the thoughts more accustomed to whispering in the shadows, and everywhere spread them in the full light of day. There are to be no more inequalities, no more castes. The threads of the intrigue tighten and each of those who have come together embraces the role entrusted to him, so that the pre-arranged concatenation of events will let the French Revolution explode.

As the tale of Cagliostro also shows, the plot comes from *somewhere else*. The outsider insinuates himself into the inner space. The agents of occult forces, the envoys of rival powers, the plotters are strangers who wander in the night, nomads who prowl around serene dwellings, nameless vagabonds who penetrate into places of prosperity to bring misery and ruin, foreigners who introduce disease and epidemics, the Jews who have spread contamination, infestation, destruction, for centuries. The spectre of the plot besieges the city, haunts its dreams, rather like the spectre of revolt. It brings the fear of ending up in unknown hands, in the manipulations of some obscure planner whose motives remain unknown. Right in the heart of the city, in some gloomy hovel, in an underground labyrinth, in a bottomless pit, lurks the Kingdom of the Plot, that web of evildoing that threatens to subjugate the entire world and become global domination.

Spokesmen for the Deceived

In the vast literature on conspiracy, Leo Löwenthal's name usually gets passed over in silence. This is just the opposite of what happens to Richard Hofstadter, who has become renowned and remembered almost everywhere for introducing the theme of paranoia into the political field. There are important factors that explain their different fortunes.

Now widely used in everyday language, 'paranoia' has become a term to stigmatise those who suffer from conspiracist delusions. But who can pass judgement? Who can distinguish between the irrational and the rational, between pathology and the norm, in the political sphere? Hofstadter speaks of a 'paranoid style' in order to indicate a certain 'fanaticism' present at the 'extremes' of both far right and far left.[1] This way of considering the opposite poles of the political space is deeply influenced by the 1950s, when Hofstadter began writing his essay *The Paranoid Style in American Politics*, though it would not be published until 1965. He prepared this work during the period of McCarthyism, in which it was necessary to show that the two apparently antithetical ideologies of Nazism and communism sprang from the same 'political psychology', followed the same patterns and produced similar outcomes. Just like the etymology of 'totalitarianism', the etymology of 'paranoid style' also establishes a barrier beyond which it is not permissible to venture; it puts up the forbidding sign that discredits any alternative in advance. Together with other more or less liberal US intellectuals, Hofstadter added to the conceptual arsenal that would serve to renew and strengthen liberalism – progressive, pluralist, tolerant – while protecting the 'sane' nation from the irrational tendencies of the two extremes, abruptly conjoined by the stroke of a pen.

Löwenthal had taken a rather different approach, though Hofstadter surely drew more than one idea from his writings. Written in English with the help of Norbert Guterman – and later republished in German – the book *False Prophets* had appeared already in 1949, firing the starting gun on the famous 'Studies in Prejudice' series edited by leading figures in the Frankfurt School.[2] It stemmed from the same context as the research, directed by Max Horkheimer and Theodor W. Adorno, which would feed into the volume *The Authoritarian Personality*.[3] These German Jews, who had escaped the Third Reich, noted disturbing signals that had otherwise been overlooked; in their exile on the other side of the Atlantic, they experienced a troubling déjà vu, as they saw a *ressentiment* that seemed liable to explode at any moment.

Löwenthal devoted his attention to the figure of the agitator who uses his techniques to manipulate the public in order to fool them into believing that they are victims of sinister, occult forces. Foreigners, immigrants, communists, traitors, and, of course, Jews – these are the enemies of America, who, like parasites, lurk within it, worming their way into it to bring disease and destruction. They are the ones pulling the strings of an elaborate plot.

The list of grievances is a long one; it ranges from general discontent to economic difficulties, from disappointed expectations to existential defeats. Taking up the guise of an advocate for change, the agitator reinforces and stiffens every sense of wounded pride, humiliation, and repressed rage, directing them outwards. After so many sacrifices, and indeed the promise of eventual reward, the dissatisfaction is enormous. Too many dreams remain unrealised. One can blame the failure on one's own mistakes, misplaced hopes, and blatant inadequacy. There are some who seek solace in religion, and some who indulge in cynicism. But if this does not happen, then the fury of disappointment is an unstoppable force. The agitator breaks the taboo that imposes optimism – 'everything's OK!' – and admits that things are not OK. He bluntly calls his followers 'losers', just like himself. He is one of them, and they can put their trust in him, because he is sincere. And because he finally says what the others will not say – that it's all a con. They have been taken in, or, rather, they have allowed themselves to be taken in. Their mistake was to be so gullible, so naive. It is time to wake up. The intellectual inferiority, the limits, which so inhibited them, can now be openly confessed, even boasted about. Surrounded by an unprecedented aura, humiliation suddenly becomes the hallmark of a new elite.

The condition of those who have been 'taken in' is a perennial one, without remedy. There is nothing the victims can do to change it, other than denounce the plot hatched by an immoral and unscrupulous enemy. Of course, this enemy cannot be seen – but only because it is hidden and covertly pursues its dark ends. However, its effects are felt. And that is enough.

Consistent with the ideas of the Frankfurt School, and in particular with a social critique using psychoanalytic or psychiatric categories, Löwenthal does not hesitate to speak of 'paranoia'. He was, indeed, the first to do so. But, at the same time, he distanced himself from the risk which Hofstadter runs, of stigmatising political opinions and behaviour considered a deviation from the norm. On the contrary, the suspicion has some justification. If there is a tendency for people to feel targeted by a threatening power, this is because, as the individual sphere of action shrinks, it appears that the world is increasingly in the hands of anonymous forces. That someone should try to grasp its developments does not mean they are paranoid. There is an indistinct boundary between the two things.

A vague suspicion can be a good starting point for an analysis of the economic and political situation. But the agitator proceeds in the opposite direction: he turns suspicion into certainty, sensation into a complete analysis. The plot becomes a distraction, which impedes the investigation of reality. Here, the world is not complex – it is complicated by deliberate machinations, a concerted sabotage. The web of the plot takes on gigantic, imaginative, cosmic dimensions. It extends through space, spreads through time and becomes immemorial. Since time immemorial, those forces have worked for destruction – it's just that they are also able to put on new masks. Hence the agitator, whipping up the intoxication that comes from lapping at this mythical source, need do no more than unveil the mystery from time to time.

The spokesman of deception is – at one and the same time – a false prophet, a ridiculous and dangerous seer who identifies trickery everywhere. But he is also the megaphone who gives voice to the plot, who amplifies an unspoken fear, an apocalyptic anxiety.

Sovereign *Ressentiment*

All our failures, setbacks, and defeats are nothing more than the perverse consequences of action by other people – the privileged, the dominant, the usurpers. It is they, plotting behind our backs, who pass off their disguised interests as absolute truths, who profit from all this immense injustice. Such is the vision worked up by the resentful. In so doing, they find an alibi to sublimate their own limitations; they devise a pretext to turn baseness into superiority, mediocrity into excellence, weaknesses into virtues, faults into merits. Nietzsche exposed this way of turning things on their head in his *On the Genealogy of Morals*.[1]

In the current scenario, *ressentiment* has taken on a political role and an existential dimension beyond anything seen in previous eras. The collapse of utopias, the withering of grand narratives, the difficulty of reading what course the world is headed on, the global crisis of progressive visions and projects for emancipation, the lack of a political language able to equip individual suffering with a common hope – all this feeds a *ressentiment* that has become almost an ordinary way of life. Everyone is left up to their own disillusionment, to their own irreparable helplessness. The pattern of these threads used to hold together the prospect of redemption; today, there instead creep in the little private grievances, narcissistic accounts, angry ruminations, the running commentary of those who must submit. In the shared distress, in the diffuse malaise, the *ressentiment* does not spring so much from the realisation that iniquities and offences exist as from the inability to overcome them by pointing to any common ideal of justice. Instead, each person senses their own powerlessness. It then becomes essential to look for some anaesthetic in order to cope with the grief and anguish. We can say that *ressentiment* wins out wherever the principle of hope falters.

It is precisely the a priori dismissal of any alternative, accused of a totalitarian inclination or perceived as a chimerical illusion, that opens the door to the phantasmatic compensation of the resentful, who imagine they will one day dominate the dominant through the wave of a magic wand. In this respect, *ressentiment* is a submissive kind of revolt. It goes no further than an alienated attempt to overcome alienation, a shortcut to overthrowing power relations. Within just moments the spark of revolt is ignited and extinguished again. The fleeting consciousness of dissent gives way to an accounting of immediate benefits. The resentful person thus ends up accepting the world he would like to exorcise. So, despite his resentful pride, he submits to the hated system and humiliates himself by paying a poorly disguised tribute to the hegemonic values he had so frantically tried to upturn. The ultimate metamorphosis is the transition from intransigent animosity to bitter resignation or – depending on how fortunate he is – to an oblivious, blithe acquiescence. This is why the party of the resentful is bound to continual erosion and splintering, the product of its repeated defections and its self-interested calculations.

The growing climate of depoliticisation has, paradoxically, made *ressentiment* more political. On closer inspection, it has been a potential component of various ideologies for decades now. To detect the ways in which it is used, we need only consider its modalities and its effects. Instead of painstakingly seeking a way out of the frustrating and grievous situation which he is forced into, the resentful person prefers an easy way out. The escape route he looks for is a sophisticated inversion of his own image, that of others and his relationship with the world. Thus, with a masterstroke, he manages to see himself in another way – that is, other than how he is, and different to how others see him. At the same time, in his rancorous purism, he vents his identitarian passion, his phobia of the other, and his refusal to grow, to change. At the existential-political level, what *ressentiment* above all asserts is the right to persist in one's own essence. Which means: not having to open oneself up to the outside world, and not adding anything – any further agony – to the pain of this humiliating situation, and still less the torment of being forced to adapt. It is better to shun and reject the changes taking place in the world, or even to deny the world itself.

Exaggerated recrimination – the only form of contact with the outside world – leads to an ethno-egoistical retreat. This is how the People of *ressentiment* takes form: through separatism, the demand to break away, isolationism, the desire to withdraw, to burn bridges, to put up walls, the need to be by oneself, among ourselves, internally, while leaving adversaries – or, rather, enemies – on the outside, so as to be free from the cold accounting of competition and to be judged only by internal values, in an economy of sovereign *ressentiment*. Within this bedrock, we can see the narrowest nationalism, the entrenchment in small nations, white supremacism, xenophobia, sovereigntist regression, and particularism.[2] Doubtless *ressentiment*, standing between nostalgia and reaction, is part of the ideology of the right, where, faced with deterritorialisation, international capital, and planetary exile, the attempt is made to restore the fetishes of nation and family, recovering the symbolic territories of stability and identity.

But *ressentiment* also crosses borders. It turns out to be an ingredient of different political ideologies. So, there is no pure ideology of *ressentiment*; rather, it is articulated in a variety of political forms. Each ideology draws to different degrees and in different ways from this inexhaustible source. There is, therefore, also a left-wing *ressentiment* – something not to be confused with the righteous anger against the world which, when channelled, directed, raised up, aims to change the world and certainly not to deny it. Conversely, *ressentiment* takes root in disillusionment. This happens where unrealistic strategies end up in blind alleys, while the world that has always been remains an insurmountable obstacle. But it also happens where searing defeats, or rather battles never fought, are stubbornly repressed in the name of governmental compromise and administrative accommodation.

Neither left nor right? Not really. While these coordinates remain valid for political orientation, *ressentiment* proves to be the source par excellence of populism, where it finds its most natural outlet. That is why, in its course, through its secondary currents and subterranean flows, it feeds that great quantity of hybrid ideologies with which the contemporary landscape is strewn: from moderate progressives to the partisans of conservative revolutions, from right-wing libertarians to left-wing sovereigntists. Demagogues and agitators – the true protagonists of the newest variants of populism, aim at a 'return to the people' – not, of course, to promote the ferment of revolt, but to cultivate recrimination and foment the protests of the resentful. As these latter rediscover popular common sense, the rough-and-ready cunning of the masses, the dear old habits of the vulgar people, they can finally vent their *ressentiment* against the elite, the 'real powers behind the scenes', the technocrats, the experts, the radical-chic intellectuals. Hence the same *ressentiment* which allows them to wallow in impotence, to sublimate their frustrated

ambitions in consoling fantasies, to anaesthetise the grief
of their disenchantment and fill in the void of anguish,
appears as the new opium of the people.

Perhaps we might better speak of tribes than of peoples.
To understand this, we need only take a look at the public
sphere, divided into opposing mobilisations, fragmented
into camps of identity and victim encampments, agitated
by unending neighbourly quarrels and family disputes,
and criss-crossed by endless hostility and a vicious *pàthos*
that feed irreconcilable desires and allow for no relations
other than ones of mutual intimidation. It is here that
ressentiment offers an ethical alibi for a neo-tribalism that
manifests and expresses itself in rancorous reinventions
and particularistic claims.

Each tribe avoids having to be confronted with other
ones, allowing it to claim an exclusive victim status.
Ressentiment – as Max Scheler argued – is not only a
spirit of revenge, deferred and perpetuated in time.[3] It is
also an expression of incapacity, of a profound impotence.
However, it is exactly this subordinate, inferior condition
that gives the right to victim status and to the denial of all
responsibility. Pure and innocent, persecuted by a cruel
and corrupt world, the resentful person sees himself as the
victim not so much of a system doomed to abjection and
imposture – for whose salvation he has no remedy – as of
a power clique that must be punished. Here are the real
culprits: it is they who are responsible.

The resentful person has a long memory; he is, moreover, tormented by constant suspicion, the sense of living
in an illusory world, and a mania for malevolent interpretation. He has a marked tendency to believe in conspiracist
versions of events, or, rather, himself fabricates them. His
flair for seeing plots and his *ressentiment* are closely connected by the same mythical logic, the same inversion of
values. In each case, the hermeneutics of the *mundus inver-
sus* plays a decisive role. The blame for this world goes as
far as the invocation of an Other World, where justice is
fulfilled. With the caveat that while, in the religious per-

spective, this means the afterlife – 'my kingdom is not of this world' (John 18:36) – in the modern conspiracist view, it means the netherworld of domination, as revealed by the penetrating gaze of the resentful.

The New World Order

Even as globalisation took hold in the years following the Cold War, it already seemed to have lost any contours, to be getting out of hand. By some strange paradox, the unification of the world by means of capital and technology produced an unprecedented and unfathomable disorder.[1]

Within such a landscape, it is no wonder that conspiracism – with its thirst for a well-ordered whole – became so pervasive, so unstoppable. What is lying behind the apparent chaos? Is the conflict of all against all, the new global civil war, not a way to rule through chaos? Who has devised the plot? Who is really in control? In the conspiracy sphere, the disturbing and terrible word 'Synarchy' has gained resonance as a name for the occult global government that manipulates nations and turns whole peoples into its slaves. Yet much more successful is the phrase 'New World Order'. Coined in 1972 by the American ideologue Robert Welch, it has been taken up so widely that it has become, along with the acronym NWO, the very symbol of the new conspiracism. The NWO helicopter, the attack force of the New World Order, flying overhead, invisible and imperceptible, is the effigy of the planetary super-plot.

This imagery feeds and intensifies the nightmare of a world made uniform, a world without borders and myths, made to conform to the same set of values and norms, a world subjected to the sole protection of a foreign, totalitarian power. Such a nightmare was already foreseen, indeed in alarming tones, by Ernst Jünger in his 1960 essay *Der Weltstaat*. The existence of the Iron Curtain – the apparent division of the globe between the two great powers of the day – did not stop him from glimpsing a growing uniformity, standing over and above nations, which everywhere spread according to the rhythm of technology and its cosmic-planetary characteristics. The zenith that loomed in the background was the world state; this was to be understood not as a rational imperative, to be arrived at by common consent, but rather the advent of an unprecedented form which the world's dizzying course seemed to be settling into and conforming to. Jünger spoke of a *Gestell*, with reference to that device that escapes control, that goes beyond the traditional concept of the state and opens up a disturbing landscape of anarchy.

If the globalised world, with its mobility, its transformations, and its sheer speed, stirs disquiet, the answer is not the reactionary closure to which Jünger alludes, namely the restoration of the state-centric order, the reappropriation of sovereignty, and the strengthening of national communities and identitarian cultures. Nor can closure be found in conspiracism. The juridical question 'Who will govern the world?', already posed by Jacques Attali, requires an in-depth analysis that, starting from the 'losers' of globalisation, turns its focus to the governance that administers the planetary economy.[2] But when complexity hardens into complication, then the answers most within reach are the ones found in the plot-producing machine, that web that has expanded its grip in both space and time.

To unearth the hidden power of the 'caste' is to expose its foreignness. The elites are especially targeted insofar as they are taken for the cutting edge of a hidden infiltration by foreigners. This is why the plot par excellence is the

'Jewish plot' – an accusation that, taking various forms, has fuelled anti-Jewish hatred over the centuries. More properly political categories are merely the translation of a religious backdrop in which the Jew is the apocalyptical enemy, in possession of a cosmic secret which bears the key to world domination.

The Jewish plot against Christian society was, especially in medieval times, built around blame for well-poisoning. This charge was most vehemently levelled during the Black Death of 1348. But to poison is to pollute, to contaminate, to infest – that is, to destroy in order to dominate. Even the local-level rumour carries within itself the denunciation of a plot, which would take on national dimensions in the modern era. We need only mention the infamous 'affair' in which Alfred Dreyfus, the young French captain unjustly indicted for high treason, was involved between 1894 and 1906. The next step – fuelled at the beginning of the twentieth century by the spread of the *Protocols of the Elders of Zion* – was the international plot, which assumed various forms: the 'Jewish-Plutocratic' plot, personified by Rothschild, Theodor Herzl's 'Zionist' plot, and, above all, 'Judeo-Bolshevism', the Red threat as represented by the left-wing Jewish intelligentsia from Leon Trotsky to Rosa Luxemburg, who could exert their grip over the world thanks to the October Revolution.[3]

Foreigners who could not be assimilated to nations, able to maintain ties among themselves across borders, exponents of both the old diaspora and the newly uprooted, the Jews are said to have woven a web around the globe, the planetary plot of the 'world Jewish conspiracy'. This becomes the supreme threat, the super-plot, the mega-plot that absorbs all past ones and contains within itself the others to come. Globalisation fuels the myth of the Jewish plot, which, as it moves from one location to another, as the image of the world expands, at the same time becomes more powerful. For it gathers its forces in the netherworld where the threads of the plot are woven, the hidden place where the Jewish people, that secret super-society specialised in crimes of infiltration and manipulation, governs the world's fate.

The accusation of constituting a 'state within a state' mirrors the accusation of weaving a planet-wide plot. Already in his day, the German philosopher Johann Gottlieb Fichte – not by accident an ardent nationalist – cast the shadow of this suspicion.[4] But even in the current scenario, this point must not be overlooked: the plot undermines domestic state sovereignty, as it strengthens the occult world government. In either case, the outsider creeps in to impose his domination.

So, we can better understand why there is today, at the same time, talk of both the 'Deep State' and the 'New World Order'. These are two sides of the same coin. These underground forces are the monstrous vehicles of globalism, which appears under all manner of acronyms: UN, IMF, NATO, ECB, WHO, NGOs, EU. It is easier to read everything with the super-symbol NWO – New World Order.

The 'Deep State' made headlines with Trump; as the impeachment proceedings against him mounted, he claimed that he had unmasked a 'big government' plot to remove him from power. Yet this is not a new term. It is a translation of the Turkish expression *derin devlet*, which, in the period between 1960 and 1980, designated that part of the secret services devoted to countering a hypothetical Soviet invasion.[5] At first, the words 'Deep State' entered into political terminology without having any conspiratorial echo; this term referred to those groups that continued to hold power regardless of the comings-and-goings of parties and governments. So, the Deep State was what undermined popular sovereignty: the power of offices, i.e. of bureaucrats and administrators who, as Weber had already pointed out, could manoeuvre in the inner folds of the state machine aided by the proliferation of norms and the excrescence of rules.[6] Their competence, which is indispensable for the functioning of this machine, is fused with expert specialisation. Increasingly complex knowledge requires expertise, preparation, and sectoral skills. He who 'knows best' can easily be recognised as he who is able to 'defend the higher interests of the nation'. The outbreak of the COVID-19 pandemic quite clearly illustrated this. We need only look to the example of Italy's Mario Draghi, the super-expert, super-banker, super-administrator. But all this conflicts dramatically with democracy. What is the point of 'government by the people' if it is always the same powerful groups that rule?

This question is not only quite fair but also necessary. The 'government of experts' takes its sovereign stand amidst the dark sphere of the exception. Blind faith in its expertise harbours unthinkable dangers. A politics that merely carries out the instructions of such expertise is erasing itself, reducing itself to an administration whose ideal is neutrality and which, indeed, no longer has any ideals of its own. No matter if the world has justice, equality, or solidarity – it only matters that it should be well administered. The functioning of the machine becomes a value unto itself, while the good politician is held to be nothing more than the highest of experts, the hyper-technocrat of planning, who at best knows how to choose the means of government but no longer knows why, or to what end – or, better, no longer knows how they ought to choose the end.

What role, then, is played by international finance, multinationals, pharmaceutical industries, military lobbies, technocracy, and managers? Once again, the shortcut of concluding that a plot is afoot leads us straight from machine to machination. The 'Deep State' will then become the hidden place where the outsider lurks, where the nation's enemies, the Decision Makers, operate unperturbed. They are said to have all manner of agendas: to confine citizens by depriving them of all freedom, to track them with microchips, to collect biometric information, to geolocate them, to spy on them with surveillance systems, to control them with mobile phones, cameras, and drugs. A submissive immersion in a uniformising world is meant to facilitate the construction of a global consensus. Social engineering is said to culminate in genetic interference: transplants, cloning, hybrid cross-breeding, steps towards transhumanism, the transference of consciousness into cyberspace, the replacement of humans by machines. The threat to the integrity of the living – the systematic trans-formation of life – is said to be the outcome of a new bio-power that casts off all limits and ushers in the reign of death, even at the level of geopolitics.

In this schema, the architects of globalisation, the engi-neers of globalist integration, in their work of eliminating borders and erasing differences, are said to be preventing all comparison and contradiction, any possibility of 'think-ing differently', any chance of a critical counter-power. The deliberate planning of crises, wars, epidemics, and bioterrorism, the organised uncertainty, the deployment of permanent threat, is held to be the factor that grants the New World Order its solidity and stability.

The 'Great Replacement' and the QAnon Patriots

Before carrying out two terrorist massacres in Christchurch, New Zealand, on 15 March 2019, in which more than fifty people lost their lives, the white supremacist Brenton Tarrant uploaded a manifesto entitled *The Great Replacement*. From its pages emerges the obsession – widespread on the far right – with the supposed extinction of European peoples, who are said to be being replaced by waves of immigrants. Many leading international press outlets, including *Le Monde*, converged in directly implicating the French writer and essayist Renaud Camus, father of the myth of the 'great replacement'. This was not, however, the only occasion on which his words brought death. Just a few months later, the attack on the Poway synagogue in California and the massacre in El Paso – the bomber had spoken of a 'Mexican invasion of Texas' – seemed to demonstrate that the idea of a 'disappearance of the white race' had by now taken hold, to the point that it catalysed widespread violence.[1]

Far from the sole preserve of extremist fringes, the myth of the 'great replacement' has been promoted in different forms – and often taken literally – by right-wing sovereigntists and neo-populists, from Salvini to Orbán, but even by leading figures of a mystifying nationalist left. Despite the condemnations that have arrived from various quarters, the imagery of 'the replacement' seems firmly established not only in public opinion but also among certain cultural voices. We need only think of Michel Houellebecq's novel *Submission*. Already formulated in the *Abécédaire de l'innocence* in 2010 and, most notably, in *Le Grand Remplacement* – first published in 2011 before appearing in several other editions – Renaud Camus' thesis is easy enough to summarise: an established people, who have occupied the same territory for more than twenty centuries, are going to be replaced in only twenty years by a people coming from outside. The 'natives' – i.e. those born on the soil where their people have always lived, a soil which they can claim as their own – are being replaced by immigrants. This is not said to be a warlike invasion, as in the past, but described as an underhand development which takes place through processes of 'alteration', 'dissolution', and 'destruction'. In this account, the identity of the original people – the French people in particular and the European peoples more generally – is thus irreversibly undermined to the point of being wiped out, thanks also to a 'demographic submergence'. Everything is said to be stripped of its origins, de-localised, de-nationalised by an 'enormous replacement machine' whereby individuals are no longer recognised as irreplaceable but made into exchangeable equivalents, by way of egalitarian ideology. 'Nocence' – harmfulness, the urge to damage – is thus said to prevail over 'innocence'.

The culprits? The 'globalist' elites who, in an acquiescent silence, propped up by media 'lies', allow and, indeed, promote a 'global replacism'. This is said to be the totalitarianism of the twenty-first century. Although Camus emphasised that the 'great replacement' is not a concept but a phenomenon, his 'thesis' is nothing more than the ideology of the plot. In catastrophic, anxiety-producing tones, the representatives of the world's overclass – i.e.

an obscure 'replacist power' – are accused of striving to break up European civilisation through a deliberate 'immigrationist' policy. Here, it is impossible not to make out – as the historian Valérie Igounet has noted – the echoes of the 'Kalergi Plan', so named after the pan-Europeanist Richard Coudenhove-Kalergi, to whom the denier and neo-Nazi Gerd Honsik in 2005 attributed the original authorship of a fantastical plan to ethnically replace white peoples.[2]

Old spectres of European history have re-emerged in the recent past. On closer inspection, the plot outlined by Camus is the latest, softened and updated version of the 'world Jewish conspiracy'. But if the author – repeatedly indicted for revisionism and incitement to racial hatred – has tried to conceal his blatant antisemitic bias, he does so only in order to circumvent more easily the public censure against it.

When we look to identify the precedents for Camus' ideas, we will surely think of Jean Raspail's apocalyptic novel *Le camp des saints*, published in 1973. It describes the 'end of the white world', as it is submerged by millions and millions of immigrants, against whom the Europeans turn out to be disarmed.

The escape route to Switzerland, where Raspail took refuge, would thus appear to be the only chance to preserve what remains of Western life. It just so happens that, at a time when fiction is becoming reality, Raspail's novel has been warmly recommended, by Steve Bannon and Marine Le Pen, as insightful political analysis.

Going back even further, it is possible to find the myth of substitution already in the writings of the Catholic journalist Éduard Drumont, the so-called pope of antisemitism, who in his 1886 bestseller *La France juive* predicted a Jewish domination which would be capable of destroying his country. Especially decisive, however, is the name of the writer Maurice Barrès, an exponent of French revanchism and an antisemitic propagandist during the Dreyfus affair, to whom we owe the very idea of *remplacement*. Renaud

Camus did not invent anything but merely cleansed the monstrous dread of replacement – a fear long established in the conspiracist imagination – of its overt antisemitism.

To prove that the Great Replacement is but a digestible adaptation (for those with poor memories) of the 'world Jewish conspiracy', we need only turn to the pages of *Mein Kampf*. Unlike nomads, who still possess some land, albeit in an indeterminate way, the Jews – Hitler argued – lead a 'parasitic' existence to the detriment of other indigenous peoples who, as soon as they manage to unmask the Jews, will expel and banish them. As Arthur Schopenhauer put it, the Jew is 'a great master of lies'. This people pretends to be something it is not; the Jews pretend to be assimilable, they convince their hosts that Judaism is only a religion. They are, however, *Fremde*, foreigners who, pursuing a clear political strategy, undermine the identity of nations from within, poison their blood, corrode their culture.[3] On the one hand they incite the anticapitalist struggle, while on the other they destroy national borders. They do all this to realise their 'global scam' – the plot for stealing power.

In the years following the Second World War, the idea that the Jews were pursuing a plan to undermine the peoples of Europe, to alter them, to drown them under a wave of 'niggers' and 'Mongols', was widely circulated among extreme right-wing circles. The idea soon spread to the United States, where, carried along by white supremacist mobilisations, it introduced the suspicion that even government authorities are, through their silence, complicit in a conspiracy that aims to erase the 'white race' in the name of multiculturalism.

From this sprang a narrative that would find one of its fullest expressions in the 1978 novel *The Turner Diaries*. Written by the neo-Nazi William Luther Pierce under the pseudonym Andrew Macdonald, this was a book that fomented violence and led to people's deaths. A clutch of supremacists, who call themselves 'patriots', storm the Capitol building in Washington with the aim of overthrowing the US government – that is, a collaborating and complicit System. Many dozens of people lose their lives in the attack, including members of Congress and their collaborators. Everything seems to end in the nothingness of those deaths. But, for the supremacists, this marks a symbolic victory: 'The real value of our attacks today lies in the psychological impact, not in the immediate casualties. More important, though, is what we taught the politicians and the bureaucrats. They learned this afternoon that not one of them is beyond our reach.'[4]

Speaking, here, is the protagonist Earl Turner – but it could have been a follower of QAnon, among those who, on 6 January 2021, to the world's astonishment, joined in the assault on the Capitol fomented by Donald Trump.[5]

Later, Pierce, a physicist who turned his hand to politics, a founder of the National Alliance, who unabashedly advocated the extermination of the Jews and other 'impure' groups, wrote *Hunter*. Published in 1989, this is a novel of much more populist tone which recounts the exploits of a war veteran who targets mixed couples and civil rights activists. The 'Jewish question' increasingly becomes that of the enemy within, of the occult power that uses egalitarian democracy to promote 'multiracial tyranny'.

The events of the new century thus reactivate a well-rooted imaginary, as they rekindle the idea that migration is the outcome of a Jewish plot to replace the 'white race' with a half-caste, hybrid, and heterogeneous humanity. In Renaud Camus' version, the adjective is removed (it is implied, anyway), so as to present migration as the 'great replacement' tacitly supported and ultimately desired by the 'global overclass'. In *Le Grand Remplacement* the conspiracist connotations remain obvious. This is especially true given that Camus himself speaks of a 'replacist power'. Anxiety and uncertainty over epoch-making changes coagulate into an identitarian sickness. After the spectre of a 'Eurabia' subject to sharia law, which raged in the first decade of the new millennium, there reappeared the terrifying, unbearable spectre of 'replacement'.

Beyond the new sovereigntist right, the idea that everything is being guided by a hidden hand has become widespread, even to the point that it holds sway over migration policies. This means reasserting the 'native' population's right to the land, denying citizenship to the children of immigrants, and leaving shipwrecked people to die. In Italy, NGO rescue ships are called 'sea taxis', while the populist chorus blames 'over-tolerant' parties for the massacres in the Mediterranean.

This is not only a shortcut explanation, by which the complex phenomenon of contemporary migration is turned into the direct outcome of an organised plot. The migrant, who ignores the existence of borders, brings a different tradition and language, and denationalises the labour force, is, in the eyes of the sedentary native, the absolute Other, the figure who crystallises all the anxieties of the globalised world. But behind this nomad once again lurks the Jew, the real manipulator. No one personifies him better than George Soros, the speculator and philanthropist, who looks kindly on the end of national sovereignty and the advent of multicultural societies, uses the press to spread these ideas, encourages progressive citizens' movements, and finances NGOs and humanitarian institutions. This exponent of the 'Deep State' then becomes the very symbol of the 'globalists' who are driving the Great Replacement.

The Extreme Taste for the Apocalypse: Hidden Enemies

Apocalyptic visions have always been attempts to interpret one's own era. Yet never, as at the beginning of the new millennium, has the 'end' – a spectre which has shaken the centuries – taken on real contours. It appears in forms ranging from global pandemics to out-of-control debt, inequities and inequalities, unstoppable migratory movements, climate collapse, resource depletion, a diffuse sense of malaise, and endless absurdities. There is a mounting sense of anticipation, filled with anxiety and apprehension. The black sun stands out in the polluted sky. The imminence of the end now has a historical and no longer merely cosmological character. We are the first to think that we may well be the last. In the millenarianisms of the past, it was possible to fantasise about the end, in the mix of beliefs, expectations, and delusions.[1] Today, amidst monstrous bio-disasters and alien invasions, the countless screens, which provide just so many mirrors of the times, reflect that epic of destruction punctuated by the extinction of the human species and the obliteration of the planet. The historical certainty of the end sets the tone for an epoch that takes the form of an apocalyptic scenario in which both theological resurrection and political hope are lacking. The apocalypse looms amidst the full development of modernity. The idea of progress runs out of steam, and faith in the possibility of influencing the course of events, avoiding the inevitable, disappears. The sufferings and abuses endured in the present find no promise of reparation in a future world of justice. Each human life becomes a story unto itself, dispersed and separated in a singular destiny, while History loses meaning and the world becomes an indecipherable intrigue.

The background of the plot is the apocalypse – understood not only in the usual sense of catastrophe but also in its original one of revelation. The world is dominated by an evil power of boundless destructiveness, a hidden, ruthless, and unscrupulous tyrannical force that inflicts torment and reaps victims. The hope is not that it can be overthrown but that it will be exposed. The veil will finally be torn away. This move will be enough to unmask the deception. Once revealed, the occult force will lose all its power. And then will come a new beginning.

At stake, here, is the world's very safety. This is indeed a cosmic plot. Its web extends everywhere in space, and it even goes back in time. Behind the scenes, manipulators tightly hold the strings, direct historical events, control human affairs. They cannot be bargained with; no concessions can be made to them. It is a matter of all or nothing. The struggle against this global enemy is titanic, a planet-wide conflict, an epoch-defining battle.

Even beyond the Manichaean strife between Good and Evil, the clash takes on apocalyptic proportions. This is a decisive point. The enemy does not threaten only a nation; he rises up against the world order, as he strives to change, undermine, and destroy this order. His victory would thus mean the end of history, the twilight of civilisation, and the death of the planet. Hence the existential hatred, the enormous *ressentiment*, the anguished tension between salvation or nothingness, the semi-prophetic passion with which the final catastrophe is spoken of.

The clash does not take place in the traditional space of conflict between states, where legal norms survive. Rather, it takes place across borders, in a metaphysical realm where there is no truce, no compromise, nor any limit to the exercise of violence. The rift is a chasm, the hostility is absolute. There is no bridge such as would allow a common basis of interpretation. The occult party of Evil, barricaded in the netherworld, remains the enemy to be eliminated, and yet proves ineliminable.

This explains why the current depoliticisation of social conflict provides the gateway to conspiracism. The two phenomena are closely related; indeed, it is quite remarkable that this has not yet been adequately noted. Today, the enemy is not the class enemy, nor that of a hostile nation. On the contrary, the enemy can be either the extremely close – such as the anonymous tenant upstairs – or the extremely distant – such as the famous 'Brussels bureaucrats'. Particularly on the web, this primary struggle – almost a battle for recognition, and for existence itself – is unleashed against a 'them' of obscure definition, which is to be insulted and attacked, an undifferentiated plural that becomes the target of all manner of destructive impulses. The alibi is always a defence against those evil forces that make life impossible. Indeed, we should not underestimate the violence of verbal attacks that, even when directed against some specified target, can barely conceal their apocalyptic undertones. Death is always looming. From the 'international finance', which bleeds resources dry, to the planetary (and perhaps interplanetary) secret organisations, which surveil and manipulate, from the 'great replacement' to paedophilia and perversity, from the 'chemtrail' poisons released by aircraft to the lethal vaccinations jabbed into our arms on the pretext of a virus: everything points to the covertly perpetrated crime, the ultimate transgression, the ultimate destruction. The plot-obsessives' logic works not only by tracing the particular to the general, in more or less undue fashion, but also and above all by reading every event in light of the cosmic mega-plot. That is why rebuttals aimed at exposing their sophisms and fallacies have no effect. The conspiracist has an extreme taste for the apocalypse. Hence the enormous success of occult themes and magical sagas. The end-of-the-world atmosphere and the penchant for liminal phenomena always resurface.

The plot-obsessive moves towards the threshold of reality, to the borders between the apparent world and the netherworld, as he defends the besieged fortress of civilisation. Embodying the elite of the far-sighted, in the vanguard of those who have opened their eyes, he spots the machination before others are able to recognise it, held back as they are by myopia and ingenuity. But the limit is always also that of time running out. The anguish is that of the final days in which events come one after another. The whole order, or rather the whole world, is at stake.

The totalitarian vocation of the plot becomes apparent in the image of the enemy – that fantastical entity in which converge the many adversaries whose plurality would raise doubts over their own cause. The Enemy is One, even when it is that undifferentiated 'they' of the system or caste. Ubiquitous and omnipresent, this enemy is the mask of faceless power. However, in the construction of the absolute enemy, which contains all past ones and all those to come, there is also a dehumanisation in which the entire universe, from the microbe to the cosmos, is mobilised. Relegated to the subhuman as well as the superhuman sphere, the enemy is not trapped in the device; he is not a prisoner caught in its gears. On the contrary, he is the great manipulator. The enemy's transcendent power makes him a free and dynamic agent, able to intervene in any time and any place. Invisible and occult, ruthless and soulless, between evil and the anti-Christ, he has demonic and terrifying traits.

The enemy, with its foreign force, takes refuge in the darkness, the lair of foul beasts. Hence, as Girardet has noted, there is a veritable 'bestiary of the Plot', which includes everything that crawls and infiltrates, all that is slithering and slimy, all that carries filth and infection: the snake, the rat, the leech, the octopus.[2] But the privileged image, in this repulsive swarm, is that of the spider; nimble, black, patient, it weaves its web, enveloping its victim until it swallows and devours him. On closer inspection, the spider's web is the very symbol of the plot, its clearest representation.

Even where the manipulator seems to have a name, he appears in an animalistic guise; his physique is monstrously transformed. Such is the case of Rothschild, the 'banker' of all bankers. In a now traditional iconography, his rapacious hand becomes an octopus capable, with its tentacles, with its thousand suckers, of immobilising the victim before vampirising him. The subhuman mask assimilates and erases the face.

What does it mean to unmask? It does not only mean attributing some phenomenon to the hidden intentions of the perpetrator. It also means stripping the veil from the enemy, bringing him out of the invisibility in which his power is ultimately hidden, making known his trickery and exposing his deceptions. This revelation exposes the aggression of the manipulator, whose identity and purpose now become public knowledge. Tearing away the veil rips open and nullifies the backstory. It has a mystical-esoteric value, as Hitler, the most perverse demystifier of conspiracies, knew well. He was, similarly, aware of the potential for mobilisation contained in that apocalyptic gesture, capable of calling for the last redemptive battle. The demystifier – that is, the spokesman of deception – is both doctor and prophet: on the one hand he heals, on the other he calls for salvation.[3]

But unmasking is, at the same time, a manifest indictment of the members of the plot – those who weave hidden webs and are now made accountable for them. Unmask, accuse, and, finally, condemn. Irrevocable, definitive, the moral condemnation is a stigma against which no appeal can be made. Whoever levels the charge that a plot is afoot thereby declares himself to be a victim. It is then understandable that he defends himself against the hidden enemy that has finally been unmasked.

Since this is always about a struggle between Good and Evil, between the forces of light and the forces of darkness, it is indispensable to secure an absolute and unconditional victory. There can be no bargaining with this merciless evil, which, if not eliminated, must at least be hunted down and driven out of the netherworld in which it operates. This points towards the spiralling demands of a victory that is as taxing as it is fantastical, which only intensifies frustration, *ressentiment*, and a sense of impotence. For the conspiracist imagination, beating the enemy is not a means to an end but an end in itself.

This is why the enemy is always necessary. Indeed, the enemy serves to coagulate and define the identity of the resentful and self-victimising group, all the more so if it is a nation of loose and precarious ties. The demystifier, the spokesman of the deceived, does not show a way out but, rather, speaks of catastrophe, presented as an inexorable scenario, by appealing to an indeterminate fear, a diffuse and nagging anguish. Thanks to these phobocratic skills, he directs and orients his audience of adepts and support-ers, his followers; he encourages them not to consider the problem and the possible solutions to it but, rather, to turn their fire on the enemy, responsible for the disaster. The community of 'us' is united in its intolerance and repulsion towards 'them', the men of the real powers behind the scenes. This elite of super-oppressors, of demonic forces endowed with an almost biological destructiveness, is an unassimilable foreign body. It is the 'internationalists', the 'cosmopolitans', the 'communists', who attack national sovereignty. Yet, communism is here only a label, behind which the most sordid activities swarm. The same applies to capitalism, which is not a system but only the clique of 'international finance'. So, it is not worth occupying the factory to fight for better wages – for it is not produc-tive capital but predatory finance capital that is at fault. This distinction, which was introduced by Nazism, is again asserting itself with great success. At the top of it all, at the head of the party of Evil, is the 'banker', the emblem in the populist imagination of all manner of robbery. As the term suggests, 'international finance' is in collusion with the internationalists. Here, in a surprising move, peeks out the 'communist banker', a Rothschild who looks like Marx, a Soros who directs the NGOs.

The very symbol of indirect domination, the 'communist banker' heads the Party of Evil, which is made up of international monopolies and foreign forces. On closer inspection, it is the Party of Foreigners. Here is the enemy troop – that of the replacists and the immigrants, the multinationals, the marauders and invaders of all kinds, the agents of technology, the perverts, those who want to undermine security, to contaminate 'our' identity. Foreigners on the outside and foreigners within the nation, they are in both cases unassimilable. Behind the web, pulling the strings, is the ultimate foreigner, hidden, invisible, and intangible, extra-human and subhuman – in short, through the few traits that are still apparent, a metaphysical Jew.

In the age of globalisation, this demonic work, in which everything is altered and contaminated, is even more difficult to unmask. The enemy resorts to the same old methods: it manipulates the press, propagates fake news, controls politicians, influences minds, controls the education system; but it also reactivates occult tricks with new formulas. Starting with the virus, the malign spirit of alienness, as abstract and immaterial as it is deadly and fatal. The alteration is thus achieved, if not with epidemic infection, then at least with a vaccination secretly directed by the big pharmaceutical firms that seek super-profits for themselves to the detriment of citizens' health. But even behind Big Pharma there are the great manipulators of the world.

Hence, politics becomes a decontamination process. Trump illustrated this well, but he is not the only example. In addition to promising to remedy the democratic chaos, he presented himself as the healer of the nation's sick body, capable of cleansing it of everything that pollutes it – 'coloured' felons, Mexican immigrants, feminists and transgender people, the disabled and the sick – and of defending it from the various hidden dangers with walls, borders, and other forms of protection. On the inside, the polemical space is simplified, the cracks are filled, the ripples are smoothed out, allowing a chasmic rift to open up between 'us' and 'them', the victims and the 'powers behind the scenes', America, pure and mystical, and the Deep State that undermines and jeopardises it. This is where QAnon takes root. The pandemic caused by the foreign virus, the hyperbolic proof of every threat, once more urges an immunitarian response that will decontaminate society.

Populism and the Plot

The people are threatened, betrayed. The suspicion fuels perplexity and distrust of political authorities and public institutions, accused of pursuing their own 'caste' interests, completely at odds with those of ordinary citizens. What has happened to popular sovereignty? Democracy turns out to be a pseudo-democracy – i.e. the simulacrum of a power exercised elsewhere and for other purposes. Behind the scenes, it is possible to detect the manoeuvrings of dark, outside forces, the workings of elites in the service of foreigners. The conspiracy is inscribed in the populist imaginary of how power works.

As is well known, populism is no recent invention and has appeared in different ways throughout history. Even the definition has been a source of heated debate in recent years. What is certain is that the term, often used in polemical tones, can become a stigma. In the public debate, 'populist' is now understood as a political style characterised by simplistic theses, crude arguments, summary judgements, and easy references to popular common sense. Many agree, however, that populism is built around the tension between the people and the elite. It is, therefore, a way of seeing society separated into two antagonistic groups: on the one hand, the corrupt and alien elite and, on the other, the one, pure, homogeneous people, whose general will politics ought to express. As Cas Mudde, one of the leading scholars of populism, has argued, it is a 'thin ideology' which, cutting across the overall divide between right and left, lends itself to being combined with other ideologies.[1]

From whatever perspective we view it, populism appears to be a formidable means of mobilising the people against the system. Appealing to *ressentiment* and mobilising a widespread anxiety, it denounces the plots, the trickery, and the corruption of the establishment, its deceptions, its unpunished and repeated frauds against ordinary folks. Especially in the latest forms of neo-populism, the central register is that of alleging plots.

This is not to say, of course, that all populism, as the vulgate would have it, is despicable or possible to read in terms of conspiracism. The Argentinean Ernesto Laclau was not entirely wrong when, back in the 1970s, he emphasised its antagonistic potential. He saw in populism a force for emancipation that could, at the same time, reintroduce conflict into a political life hollowed out by a phantom consensus, and thus lead to radical democracy.[2]

But, in the current scenario, the simplification of conflicts has ended up reducing them to the Manichaean clash between the dominant and the dominated, the swindlers and the swindled, the people and the elite. The demonisation of the elite has gone hand in hand with an exaltation of 'the people' in the sense not of the plebs or the proletariat but, increasingly, as a community of origin and destiny. Not *démos*, but *éthnos*. This is the slippery path from a rebellious populism to an identitarian populism, in which the people is called upon to defend its homogeneous substance and its everlasting identity.[3]

The monistic conception of the corrupt, power-holding elite sets it in opposition to the integral, integralist idea of the authentic people, an uncorrupted and incorruptible

community. The separation is clear-cut; the rupture has
the air of purification and salvation. The dividing line also
demarcates who belongs and who does not. The people not
only claims a monopoly on the general will, supposed to
be transparent and unmediated, but also claims to impose
boundaries under the banner of identity. There is no crack
in the edifice, no difference, no dissent that can affect the
homogeneous substance of the people. Around the mys-
tique of its intangible body, the dream of a community
totally reconciled with itself, the anti-politics of the new
populism takes form. For what sense would politics have,
faced with the totalising, compact unity of the people?

As *démos* slides towards *éthnos*, *éthnos* slips and turns
its sights on the outside world. The hyper-democratic aspiration (citizens' initiatives, referendums, direct democracy)
becomes a hypo-democratic disillusionment, which aims
to expose the chaos and fraud of the democratic system.
Anger and indignation are directed not against the ruling
class but against the elite that rules from within, taking its
orders from outside. This is how 'international finance'
and the 'immigrant invasion' turn out to be the two faces
of the power against which the new nationalist, or, rather,
nativist populism, rages. This latter raises the banner of
identity and advocates exclusion: citizenship only for
natives, rights only for citizens. This call for 'nationals first'
translates into the politics of a providential state that protects the 'included', that defends the ethnic community and
the integral cohesion of its own culture and values against
globalised capitalism, globalism, and all that, coming from
outside, corrupts, alters, and contaminates. When a populist comes to power, the question does not change – in
fact everything becomes even clearer.[4] From Chávez to
Bolsonaro, from Orbán to Trump, the populist in government identifies with the 'people', is its direct spokesman,
he who protects it from the dark forces manoeuvring in the
shadows, who is not afraid to reveal the plot. The Chinese
virus, imperialists, foreigners, homosexuals, Jews – these
are the enemies, the superpowers of globalisation, the

technocrats, the world elites, those nefarious and harmful forces that are destroying the 'people'.

Xenophobia and conspiracy, aspects of the same aversion to what is external and foreign, come together in the self-defence of the immunitarian democracy that separates the protected and immune within from the exposed outside. Just as totalitarianism was in the twentieth century, so in the twenty-first century conspiracist populism is the auto-immune and destructive form that democracy has taken on, in a dizzying whirlwind of self-destruction.

Victimhood and Political Powerlessness

Those who denounce plots do not only tear away the veil, pointing the finger at the alleged perpetrator, or call for mobilisation against that enemy. More than that, they declare themselves to be victims. This further step is usually overlooked. This means glossing over the complicity between victim status and the conspiracist outlook. Only by looking at the foundations of this otherwise elusive relationship is it possible to understand the spread of conspiracism in its new forms.

The victim's breakthrough into the public space is a recent phenomenon. Through different historical conjunctures and paths which have ultimately converged, the victim's presence on this stage has been growing since the middle of the last century. In the past, the victim did not appear interesting as such; her suffering, her trauma, her wounds generally went unnoticed; they were nowhere near as significant as the violence thereby perpetrated against the community. The crime had to be fought not so much because it wronged the victim herself as because it undermined order.

A new chapter began, however, with the two world

wars. Not only did a vast number of civilians lose their lives but, most importantly, the violence culminated in genocide. There was now heightened sensitivity to the discrimination suffered by women and the most vulnerable. The victim's breakthrough onto the stage of history would have many political, ethical, legal, and intellectual effects. Not only did it dissolve the boundary between the private sphere, where pain had hitherto been processed, and the public sphere, where reparation is demanded before the eyes of everyone. Rather, the rise of the victim signalled the crisis of institutions and the weakening of the state, whose sovereignty appeared to have been undermined. It would now be preferable to speak of the victim rather than of the combatant, now that sacrifice for the fatherland no longer seemed to make sense. Humanitarian organisations are one point of reference for those who have suffered violence and persecution; they not only replace the state, which is no longer the ultimate guarantor, but they often level accusations against it. Moreover, the justice demanded by victims transcends national borders. The erasure of old limits and the opening up of new political spaces is matched by the emergence of a figure who, having long remained almost invisible, is instead taking on a decisive role in contemporary modernity.

The victim asks for nothing more than recognition – that which has been denied for so many centuries. If violence was previously considered in terms of its author, i.e. the violence perpetrated, the changed perspective instead focuses attention on the persecuted, the survivor, the defenceless person who suffered the crime. Beyond the penalty inflicted on the perpetrator, the victim, their heirs or relatives demand not only the punishment of the offender but also recognition of their own individual or collective lived experience and reintegration into the community. Having been humiliated, the victim in fact risks also suffering further discrimination. That is why they plead not so much for compassion as for acceptance.

This picture would not be complete, however, if we did not add that the victim's presence in the public space can be the source of a political turn. It is not only a matter of the individualised narration of one's suffering, of one's own drama, which asserts that point of view alone and which – if things go to court – can be an obstacle to a fair trial. The same could be said, moreover, for the case of the Court of History. But the crux of the matter is eminently political and lies in the temptation to play the victim.

Abuse, excess, most often results in the arrogation of a role that, on closer inspection, belongs to others. The competition between victims, the contest for the primacy of suffering, is a now near daily spectacle. But what sense can this victimisation actually have? In the context of intermittent and widespread violence, with its ever-growing number of risks, it is inevitable that we feel continuously exposed. This is especially true given that the state – even as it promises protections that it cannot deliver – allows the stoking of fears that make it easier to rule over an inward-looking and passive community. Phobocracy – i.e. the power exercised through systematic emergency, the extended state of alarm – may be the key term for understanding the new neoliberal governance. In such a situation, often intensified by its echoes in the media, it is not difficult to understand why everyone feels like a potential victim. This is accompanied by mistrust and suspicion of institutional authorities that appear to be unfit for purpose, incapable or entirely absent.

The emergence of the victim thus points to the depoliticisation of the public space. Each person, feeling himself to be a possible target now that he is accustomed to threat and feels an extreme sense of insecurity, pre-emptively declares himself a victim. This is also a step towards claiming rights that are often recognised and granted through this victim identity. This is, therefore, a demand not only to be protected but also to expand one's own sphere of influence in the public space. In short, the victim today has an unprecedented power.

However, in the end this is always a negative power, characterised by what the victim has been deprived of, what he has lost or suffered. It is precisely because of this role of interdiction and prohibition that the victim surrenders himself to powerlessness, in which he actually ends up entrenching himself. In this way, he endorses a logic that is both destructive and self-destructive: on the one hand it contributes to the hollowing out of politics, but on the other hand it leads the victim to mount his struggles in a labyrinth ever more populated with spectres. In this respect, too, the plot is closely connected with the victimised condition. Fredric Jameson rightly spoke of a 'poor person's cognitive mapping'; by this he means such a person's (but also the uninformed person's) means of finding their way through the complex landscape of advanced capitalism, which ends up by uncovering secret societies and secret agents rather than dealing with the real oppressors.[1] In this sense, the plot is a political diversion.

On the 'Heresy' of Believers in Plots: A Critique of Umberto Eco

As with other complex phenomena that are shaking contemporary democracy, the obsession with plots can be viewed from different perspectives. It can be understood either as an obscure yet eloquent symptom of a deeper crisis or as the relic of an obscurantist past that must simply be condemned. In the latter case, sarcastic and reproachful tones alternate in the bid to delegitimise that unrealistic, backward mindset that, while it may resurface from time to time, has no chance of prevailing. Such a perspective, which is the more simplistic and reassuring of the two, is usually the one that meets with immediate agreement and applause.

Perhaps the most authoritative exponent of the dominant anti-conspiracism is Umberto Eco. If we consider his enormous output with due attention, it is clear that the critical pages he devotes to this theme are only few. They are to be found in the essay *The Limits of Interpretation*, from 1990, and in the collection *Pape Satàn Aleppe: cronache di una società liquida*, from 2016. Also decisive, however, is his universe of novels, which not only exhibit a measure of critical thinking which appears in between the lines – which remains implicit, as far as necessary – but also unfold around the pattern of a vast plot. This appears as an atavistic error, a deviance from time immemorial that threatens to hijack the course of history and undermine Western culture. For Eco, the outdated yet still seductive belief in the plot is the expression of a profound irrationality, the emblem of a regression of civilisation.

The conspiracist heresy appears as the plot already of Eco's first novel *The Name of the Rose*, published in 1980: it is the dark background to the mysterious deaths that keep happening in the apparent peace of a Benedictine abbey in northern Italy. But it leaves its mark yet more decisively on his 1998 novel *Foucault's Pendulum*, which Eco perhaps considered his true masterpiece, and finally *The Prague Cemetery* of 2010. Other titles could be mentioned as well as these more significant examples. What is certain is that, within the folds of his novels, which are obviously open to other readings, Eco launches an attack with the intention of discrediting any conspiracist heresy and warning his readers of the grave danger it carries.

In many respects, Eco's approach is not particularly original. In fact, he crosses paths with Popper in arguing that the thirst for plots is a reaction which seeks to compensate for the void left in the Western imaginary by the disappearance of the idea of God. There does not seem to be any power to guarantee Good any more, nor, above all, one able to answer for Evil. It would seem that this incomplete secularisation leaves contemporary society vulnerable by exposing it to irrationality. The belief in plots could then be seen as a superstition capable of relieving this society of all responsibility.

However, Eco goes further. He sees in conspiracism the most dangerous phenomenon of modern irrationality; he links it to ancient Hermeticism and Gnosticism, of which he takes it for a posthumous resurgence. But why? How could a philosophical-religious current such as Hermeticism and a combination of initiatory doctrines such as Gnosticism, both of which flourished in the

Greco-Roman world, be ancient prefigurations of today's thirst to find plots?

Eco lays blame on those who worshipped Hermes, the volatile and ambiguous god, father of all the arts but also protector of thieves, in whose myth the principles of identity, non-contradiction, and the *tertium non datur* are denied, while the causal chains wind back in endless spirals. The Hermetics appear from one book to another, in their obsessive interpretation of an evasive truth and in the spasmodic search for the secret threads in which 'everything is held'. Even more severe is the judgement he casts against the Gnostics who, convinced that they have been 'thrown' into a world springing from evil, lose themselves to a sense of mistrust and alienness. Because they feel exiled, uncomfortable, they develop a contempt for those who do not feel the same negativity, and they imagine that they have a task equal to that of the superman. Both the Hermetics and the Gnostics are called into question because 'in an age of political order and peace' – that is, that of the Roman Empire, where all peoples 'seem united by a common language and culture' – the adepts of each of these sects irrationally contest that order.[1] If the Hermetics indulged their dreamlike illusion of changing the world, the Gnostics harboured a desire to annihilate it.

So, on the one hand we have deconstruction and, on the other, destruction. Eco directs his arrows against the new Hermetics and new Gnostics, with which he identifies the exponents of the cultural, philosophical, and political currents that prevailed in the years in which he was writing, from structuralism to hermeneutics. On the other hand, there is no lack of explicit references to Nietzsche, Heidegger, Deleuze, Foucault, Gadamer, Derrida, Chomsky, and so on. Here, then, is a postmodern, irrational, and anti-scientist culture, which undermines confidence in progress and challenges the order of a peaceful era built on unity. Yet this time it is a matter not of the *pax romana*, whose violence and oppression Eco has apparently repressed but, rather, of the *pax democristiana*

– that is, the peace imposed under Italy's post-1945 Christian Democracy. The background to this is an Italy shaken by the murder of Aldo Moro, extreme political conflicts, but also terrorist attacks, attempted coups, and appalling massacres, over which there looms the shadow of captured secret services.

But beyond Eco's judgement on that era – and the rather questionable instrumental move with which he assimilates two past approaches to present-day realities – the problem lies in the stigma of 'irrationality' with which he brands plot-mongering and its supposed prefigurations in the past. What does reason mean for Eco, and what rationality does he appeal to? What are the criteria by which he can say he distinguishes between real plots and the syndrome of plot obsession?

In Eco's novels, this basic attitude remains – it is just that fiction takes the place of denunciation and it is fictional characters who reveal the traits of the Hermetic–Gnostic irrationality of conspiracism. Not only is there Simonini, the archetype of the inveterate hater and forger, who draws up the *Protocols*, the gospel of modern antisemitism. More emblematic is Belbo, the protagonist of the novel *Foucault's Pendulum* (a title about which much has been written), who is the spectator of a world where no action seems possible any more. Driven by impotence and frustration, he ends up turning to heterodox beliefs and entering into exoteric and sectarian circles. His friends Casaubon and Diotallevi are also caught up in a kind of stubborn occultism, which leads them to believe in the existence of a plot. But the three eventually succumb, destroyed by their own visionary temptations, by the reckless evocation of the false becoming real and the real becoming false. Behind their visionary apocalypse stands the Apocalypse of the Italian and European 'years of lead'.[2]

The plot that forms the background to his debut novel *The Name of the Rose* is inspired by the prophecies narrated in the *Book of Revelation*. If the old monk Jorge da Burgos can sprinkle poison on the fatal manuscript –

the last remaining copy of the second book of Aristotle's *Poetics*, dedicated to comedy and laughter – it is because, in the light of his conspiracist beliefs, he feels that he is only the author, not the culprit, of those multiple deaths already written into a divine plan. The holy blends into the profane in a failed secularisation and an unaccomplished modernity: this is how Eco solves the enigma of every plot.

An accusing finger is pointed against the radical left, that of the Gnostic plot-mongers who – gripped by an apocalyptic delirium capable of turning into destructive madness – await the 'final event that will bring about the overthrow and subversion of the world and its regenerative catastrophe'.[3] But the blame is directed not only against the radical left but also against the culture and philosophy that underlies it and in which Eco claims to discern, at least in embryonic form, the conspiracist heresy.

As a modern variant of an ancient obscurantism, as a repression of civilisation, as a regurgitation of a pre-rational stage, for Eco this heresy is to be condemned in the name of rationalism – first in the name of its Enlightenment version and then in that of positivistic rationalism. This would be the only admissible line in Western evolution, which, despite irrational deviations, goes on in the name of the techno-scientific ideal. It does not matter that there are crises caused by the very rationality that has made the world illegible. Eco firmly believes in progress; in his fatalistic conception of history, there is no room for dissonant irrationalities.

An official voice of moderate progressivism, which emerged victorious in the Italy of 'opposed extremisms', a shrewd interpreter of the spirit of the age, that of a conformist and pacifying repression (in the Freudian sense), Eco makes humanistic culture a playful activity, an erudite pastime, at the end of which the rationality of the status quo is reaffirmed, only possible to improve here and there. Conspiracism becomes the enemy number one as heir to the philosophy of suspicion, which Eco sees as so much smoke in the eyes.

So, this anti-conspiracism may seem good-natured, but it is basically rigid. It is not well able to indicate a way of considering the phenomenon in its complexity and of seeking a way beyond it.

Transparency and Secrecy: In the Press

The desire for transparency permeates democracy from the bottom up, sustains it and at the same time troubles it. To clarify, to shed light, to unveil, to unravel, to decipher, to resolve – to finally arrive at the truth. No more mysteries, lies, manipulations. What appears to be the case will be perfectly in line with reality. And any suspicion will be superfluous.

Conspiracists are militants committed to transparency. Contrary to what one might suppose, they do not flee into superstition, they do not escape into irrationality, but are instead hyper-rational and turn out, on closer inspection, to be the most extreme heirs of Enlightenment ideals. Everything that is hidden must be brought out into the open. The occult, the arcane, the hidden no longer have any reason to exist. What is more: all mystery must be abolished. To put it bluntly (and with the usual Manichaeism): Good is the regulative principle of transparency and Evil that which hinders it. Evil means the corrupt elites, the occult forces, the mystifying media. After all, power resides in secrecy.

It was Georg Simmel who emphasised, in an important

1908 essay, the ambivalent effects that secrecy can have in social life. In this regard, one cannot help but recall that the Latin *secretum* comes from *secernere*, which means to set aside, to separate, to exclude; what is secret is separated, secluded, tucked away and, in this sense, kept hidden. Simmel emphasises what he calls the 'attraction' of the secret, which always confers something exclusive, grants some exceptional position.[1] The prestige of the secret, the credit it enjoys and the influence it exerts do not therefore depend on its content, which could in fact also be empty. The further step – Simmel adds – is a typical error, a systematic reversal, whereby to most people's eyes every superior figure must have some secret. It is assumed that those with power have some further, hidden knowledge. Hence the secret is execrated, demonised. Yet here it is not the secret that is connected with evil, but evil with the secret. The wicked, the immoral, the dishonest try to hide themselves; however, the reverse is not true.

We can see, then, why the secret is, on the one hand, a barrier and, on the other, a perpetual incentive to break it. The temptation to transgress, to profane, to disclose, is already part of the attraction of secrecy. But the urge to disclose increases to a hyperbolic degree in democratic society. Transparency, held up as a value and norm, can no longer tolerate any margin of obscurity or any remnant of opacity. This is where conspiracism takes root, with its promise to erase every mystery at a stroke, to unravel every enigma immediately. It is enough to penetrate into the heart of the secret to make it disappear. This is possible thanks to the plot, which, once its schema has been proven, guarantees absolute clarity. This desacralisation is wholly in keeping with the spirit of modernity, the more or less explicit obligation not to hide anything, the unconditional imperative of 'publicity'.

But the attempt to bring everything to light ends up having the opposite effect. Behind every plot which is unveiled, it can be assumed that there is some plot even better hidden. As the mystery resurfaces, the shadow of the invisible continues to loom. No longer, however, in the divine beyond, but in human space, which is populated by spectres, menacing figures, evil enemies. All invisibility is condensed in power, which is by definition occult. In this way, the information society feeds the imaginary of the secret society. Every revelation unearths enigmas which remain to be unravelled. Information becomes a machine that produces a deeper darkness. For the demand for revelation is inexhaustible in a world that has not yet been able to bid farewell to the unsolved. Only the certainty that there is a plot can dispel all doubt and interrupt the spiral. Normative transparency is, therefore, the other side of the coin of conspiracism.

The illusion of having identified the key to the problem, of finally having got to the bottom of the enigma, soon gives way to bitter disenchantment and frustration. Instead of becoming an orderly and legible universe, the world seems again to descend back into chaos. Absurdity and non-sense prevail, while unspoken words, grey areas and unanswered questions crop up everywhere. It is in this gap between the dream of transparency and reawakening in the dark course of events, between the mirage of immediacy and the shock of opacity, that belief in the plot flourishes and thrives.

The bewildered and disorientated citizen, who cannot disentangle himself from the growing complexity, who cannot sift through and interpret the enormous flow of information with which he is hit, ends up being a potential conspiracist. There is too much data, too much news, and a baffling whirlwind of different, not infrequently opposing versions. Who to believe? Certainly not the 'official version', that of the media in connivance with the 'powers behind the scenes', the accomplices of those 'occult forces' which are the cause of all evil, which have, if anything, every interest in covering up any investigation and concealing their own responsibilities. To discover the truth behind all this, it is necessary to go beyond the 'official disinformation'. Whoever stops at that is merely naive. 'You know they are lying to us,' 'you know they only tell us one side of the story,' 'you know they hide the most important things from us.'

The honest, vigilant citizen devotes himself to alternative information, devotes himself to the inexhaustible deciphering of what is going on in the world. He takes on the role of the incorruptible investigator, the upstanding counter-expert, the truth-seeking hero. Thus, this new Sherlock Holmes, able to resist all flattery, fending off all manipulation, ventures into the dark underworld of political and media power. He fulsomely embraces a police-like view of the world; he strains his ears and sharpens his gaze so that he will not miss any clues. He chances his hand not only as a detective but also as an economist, a virologist, climatologist, dietician, historian, geopolitics expert, and connoisseur of international affairs. At the end of the day, 'expertise is nothing but an invention of the elites to gag ordinary people.' And he, of course, does not fall into the trap. He is more discerning, courageous and lucid than other people are – he is ready to unabashedly raise his voice in denouncing the 'system', the 'powers behind the scenes', the 'New World Order'. Somewhat immodestly, he even confesses to himself that exhilarating feeling of belonging to an enlightened aristocracy. The dizzying narcissicism of his dissent sets him ablaze: he feels that he has been entrusted with a sacred mission. He seeks the Truth against everything and everyone, night and day. And he waits to pierce the veil.

Amidst dreams and delusions of omniscience and omnivigilance, he never misses an investigative programme, he loves noir and detective stories, fiction that goes against the grain, and alternate reconstructions of history. He steers well clear of the mainstream newspapers, to avoid being manipulated, and he is quick to get online to start a blog where he can have his own space where he can publish, without taboos, documents that others would like to remain secret, irrefutable evidence of what had already been suspected. Everything makes sense. The number of followers grows.

However, this alleged free thinker, who runs no risks other than possible ridicule, often seems to be an innocuous whistleblower, yet is one who spreads uncontrolled rumours, encourages witch hunts, feeds trial by media, and invents scapegoats. He prefers natural remedies to official medicine; vaccines make him shake his head. And of course he downplays or denies the Holocaust. He can go so far as to promote real hate campaigns, even to the point of endangering other people's lives.

So, is this free thinking or, rather, a caricature of it? This conformist in non-conformism almost always shares in commonplace banalities, which he promotes as if their argument was proven. The pleasure of repetition makes him an insatiable consumer of plots and micro-plots – a reassuring consumption, which he thus succeeds in encouraging. His doubts over method, which have little to do with Descartes, are a strategic posture. Believing everything and believing nothing are two sides of the same coin. Behind the mask of the hyper-sceptic lies the hyper-believer. As Marc Bloch observed: 'skepticism on principle is neither a more estimable nor a more productive intellectual attitude than the credulity with which it is frequently blended in the simpler minds.'[2] The conspiracist is locked in his own unsuspected doubt, which is his foundation and *raison d'être*. More than a critical spirit, he is an archaic prophet; more than an heir of the Enlightenment creed, he is an adept of occultism precisely because of his obsession with tearing away the veil that hides the truth. And occultism – as Adorno noted – is 'the metaphysics of fools'.[3]

This is not to disapprove of or reject transparency. On the contrary, this is a legitimate need and a transversal value. In the age of ties that criss-cross the planet, in which mutual trust is being severely tested, there is no one who does not applaud the clarity, perspicuity, and sharpness that ought to permeate interpersonal relations as much as economic, political, and institutional ones. Indeed, on this point we need only consider the exceptional results achieved in recent years.

On several occasions since 2008, the Swiss Leaks, the Panama Papers and the Paradise Papers have brought to light tax evasion and the shady dealings of finance capital. In 2010, the publication of 91,000 military documents shed light on the West's dirty war in Iraq and Afghanistan, a trail of lies and atrocities. That is not to mention the secret dossiers released in 2011, which revealed to the world the legal monstrosity and the human shame of the camp at Guantánamo Bay. The tireless work carried out by the International Consortium of Investigative Journalists, the network of reporters and media from almost all over the world, has exposed the cartels of multinationals, money laundering and drug trafficking by criminal organisations, arms smuggling, and all kinds of humanitarian crimes. But, above all, it has exposed the unbearable duplicity of politicians, by casting a shadow of shame on all those who take advantage of the common good for their own benefit.

It is good, then, to open up the corridors of power to citizens, so that everything is accessible and visible. We know that power cloaks itself in secrecy, hides behind the veil of the arcane, seeks refuge in the shadow of what is hidden. So let us welcome the digital wind of information that is blowing, unstoppable, through immaterial cables, dissipating the fog, sweeping away darkness, illuminating everything.

Reporters, activists, and whistleblowers have made transparency – or, as English speakers would say, accountability – their battle cry. Among them is Julian Assange, who with WikiLeaks, and the publication of millions of documents hitherto kept under lock and key, has had all manner of consequences. Beyond the man himself – the anarchist cybermilitant, and his emblematic existential and political choices – a question mark still hangs over the very way in which information is to be understood.[4] The basic idea is that power, in the form of world governance, is a plot and that the only possible strategy of countervailing power is a counter-plot that can be realised through the denunciation of imposture and the systematic revelation of elites' secrets. But it is hard to believe that, in the long run, this sort of counter-agency of the people will produce the desired results. It is not enough to unmask, to make available to everyone, secret information and data which most of the time remains decontextualised and illegible. What are they to do with it? The danger is that an important means of struggle will be confused for the end itself. Clearly, this is not how things really work.

A Manichaean view of transparency can lead to distortions. What appears to have an emancipatory potential turns out to be an instrument of domination. He who watches discovers that he is being watched. The citizen who dreams of total enlightenment runs the risk of becoming a subject exposed to permanent suspicion, subjected to a regime of uncontrolled visibility, to a panoptic surveillance, where everyone is handed over to an inquisition.

Moving through the translucent crystal palace is not so easy. One runs the risk of bumping into invisible walls. Transparency is deceptive. The dream becomes a nightmare. Even the most lucid and enlightened followers must recognise that the fideistic belief in the high heaven of transparency – as Vladimir Nabokov warns in his masterpiece *Transparent Things* – can only dazzle them.

The zealous apostles of absolute transparency must be opposed, as Baruch Spinoza did, by the right to secrecy (*Tractatus theologico-politicus*, XX). In politics, as in existence. This is perhaps the most ineliminable right in a democracy.

But the myth of transparency can also be detrimental because of the simplistic view of truth that it conveys. It presumes to dispense with all mediation, to imagine a relationship of immediacy: the gaze sticks to the image, the intellect conforms to reality. The veil is torn away. It would then be possible to grasp objective Truth with one's own hand, put it in one's pocket, as if it were an exclusive possession. The real world would be reproduced, indeed perfectly duplicated. All mediation would be superfluous, or rather harmful.

In this way, the role of the media is put into question, and indeed fundamentally contested. This is in fact what happens: it is said that the entire press is a fraud, all information channels are manipulated. It is thus necessary to beware of mystification, to protect oneself from deception, from the continuous distortion of reality, from covert persuasion. It is better to migrate to the web, to access sources directly, to make up one's own mind. Unfortunately, however, it is precisely there that deception and manipulation are lying in wait.

The naive way of understanding power is also visible in this consideration of the press. It is as if immediacy were really possible, and as if mediation were not always necessary. Of course, the media do not provide direct access to reality; if they promise to do so, either they are in bad faith or they are self-denying. Mystification exists when the sources of funding are passed over in silence and when, above all, someone boasts of a neutrality that can never materialise.

There is no single great Truth betrayed by the postmodern relativism guilty for the fake news that infests the web. As Stanley Fish aptly explained in an article for the *New York Times*, fake news arises because of the lack of mediation, of a filter.[5] Without an interpretative context, we get only 'innumerable bits (like Lego) available for assimilation into any project a clever verbal engineer might imagine; and what you don't have is any mechanism that can stop or challenge the construction project or even assess it.' Thus the news coming from a teenager's blog would appear to be much more reliable simply because it is unmediated. The mistrust of major newspapers and accredited sources has disastrous results, yet ones which have not yet been well understood. It arises from the political disintegration of the interpretative community and, in turn, contributes decisively to this disintegration.

In Praise of Suspicion

Can we try to resist the ever-spreading conspiracist disease by taking the pill of critical thinking? It is hardly obvious that this should be the case. The books, essays, and articles which conclude – and they are the vast majority – with a definitive condemnation of conspiracism, ultimately point the finger at critical theory, so-called postmodernism, deconstruction, the hermeneutics of suspicion, and – why not? – suspicion itself. If fake news is circulating, if post-truth dominates, if pseudo-news, misleading or completely invented information is easily spread, then this must be because we can no longer distinguish true from false. This is said to be the fault of those who, following Nietzsche to the letter, thought that 'there are no facts, everything is . . . our opinions.'[1] Adorno, Horkheimer, and the Frankfurt School – who were the first, moreover, to begin reflection on propaganda, totalitarianism, and the authoritarian personality – may perhaps be spared. The focus instead shifts to subsequent thinking, to certain developments in Marxism, psychoanalysis, and philosophy.

'Human science as conspiracy theory': Martin Parker published an article under this eloquent title, already clearly asserting the bind of complicity.[2] This thesis was destined to circulate, in more or less implicit form, above all in the Anglo-American context; there, 'postmodernism' would be called into question because of the disenchantment, distrust, and relativistic perspective which it is said to bring with it. In short, conspiracism is said to be the sick fruit, the perverse outcome of that detachment from the 'real' that is characteristic of postmodern narratives.[3] Elsewhere, too, this connection is taken up and read in a way that is not only cultural but also political. Thus, Bruno Latour remarks wryly on the label that he thinks he can associate with 'conspiracy theories': they are 'Made in Criticalland'.[4] It can be added that Boltanski's book, written in 2012, is an attempt not only to distinguish between those who instrumentalise a false plot and those who denounce a real one but also to defend that sociology which could be accused of conspiracism.[5] The risk is that, with such an accusation, any critique can be silenced.

The nub of the question surely lies in suspicion and its proper use. Look with distrust, do not believe in the first version of the facts, question the sources and their supposed neutrality, interpret them by peering behind and beyond. All this is an indispensable exercise in exegesis and judgement; it is, after all, what the Marxist critique of capitalism already teaches.

As is well known, suspicion became a philosophical category during the twentieth century, after Paul Ricoeur introduced his successful formula concerning Marx, Nietzsche, and Freud. In 1965 he would speak of a 'hermeneutics of suspicion'.[6] What these three seemingly distant master-thinkers have in common is the 'de-mystification' that is directed not only at the object – seeking to assert its own 'objectivity', starting with the truth – but also, and even more so, at the subject. The Cartesian philosopher doubts everything, but not his own conscience, which is, on the contrary, taken as a source of certainty. The three master-thinkers, on the other hand, each according to a different register, insinuate doubt into the Cartesian fortress. There is no immediacy any more, not even for the conscience, which does not perceive anything directly; criss-crossed by an inescapable alienness, it cannot fail to recognise itself as being forever conditioned, influenced, manipulated. Are dreams, illusions, and hopes really its own?

This question is the prerequisite for an ever-tighter and sharper critique of the complex device of power, of its microphysical repercussions on the self, on relations with others, on the world. There should, then, be less ingenuity, less false consciousness, less deceptive innocence, and more circumspection, caution, and shrewdness. Such is the orientation indicated by the 'hermeneutics of suspicion'. This does not at all mean – as some may claim, or believe – a reckless dismissal of reality, the dizzying nihilism of a dissolved and dissolute self, a polarisation of the truth that breaks down into a variety of opinions that are all equally valid. Such a way of denigrating hermeneutics – but ultimately also suspicion itself – is purely tendentious. It is generally taken up by those who would have us believe that they have exclusive possession of the true Truth, the one that is real and in accordance with the facts, and therefore refuse to seek out the truth through engagement with others. Such positions of presumptive authority, which are at times crude and naive, at other times insidious and despotic, are to be mistrusted.

Today, more than ever, suspicion must be defended, indeed praised. This is not the same as reifying it, as is the case with the doubt of the hyper-sceptic who ends up becoming overly credulous. To practise unlimited suspicion is to end up in the conspiracist spiral of the paradigm of circumstantial evidence, in the obsession with the clue taken as proof, with the trace mistaken for substantiation. Existence then becomes an exhausting enquiry, ever awaiting some definitive answer which could put an end to all questions. Everyone suspects everyone, mistrusts and fears, sees spies and informers everywhere, in a paranoid universe like the one masterfully devised by Soviet writers such as Mikhail A. Bulgakov. Denunciation alone seems to offer a way out. But, in this lucid and tireless investigation, one does not distrust one's own distrust and fails to suspect one's own suspicions.

Falsely elevated to dogma, to a non-negotiable postulate, to an unquestionable principle of life, suspicion becomes the prison into which the supposedly free spirit walls itself, somewhere between a deceitful bad faith and naive credulity. This cannot, however, be imputed to hermeneutics, deconstruction, or critical theory, which are also the antidote to conspiracism.

It should instead be recognised that hyperbolic suspicion, this interruption of mutual trust, whereby in an extreme and ruthless competition everyone feels vulnerable, exposed to every possible misfortune, without being able to count on the help of others, stems from market society. It derives from the widespread precarity, from an ever-spreading uncertainty, from systematic phobia, the domain of fear that characterises neoliberal governance.

Beyond Anti-Conspiracism

To call someone 'obsessed with uncovering plots' is surely no compliment. On the contrary, it is a stigmatising label, which can act as a strategy of exclusion, disqualifying the interlocutor and delegitimising dissent.[1] For proof of this, we need only note that no one would claim this label for themselves. That is, unless they leap to deny this in order to pre-emptively neutralise all accusations, for instance: 'I am no conspiracy theorist, but. . . .' In the end, the conspiracist is always someone else. We cannot then disagree with Noam Chomsky, who was among the first to sound the alarm on the misuse of this term.[2] The derogatory tones underlying 'conspiracist' undermine others' credibility, ridicule their point of view, and thus banish them from the public space by excluding them from the realm of 'rational discourse'. It almost goes without saying that the stigma affects those on the other side of the barricade and is generally levelled by those who, consciously or unconsciously, side with the 'official version' of events.

At this point, it is generally easiest to invoke the criteria of truth and falsity, insisting that it is possible to distinguish between them by means of objective rules and principles, and thereby avoid any misunderstandings and disputes. In this sense, many claim that 'conspiracy theories' are so called because they refer to imaginary plots that never existed in reality, and which have only been conjectured or even fabricated from scratch. They would, then, be more or less like fake news. Examination of the facts becomes crucial here. It is supposed that the findings will remove any room for doubt and silence even the most recidivist conspiracists, who stubbornly denounce the 'official version'. But that is not how things really are – and not only because of the conspiracists' stubbornness.

In fact, it is always easy to sift out the true and the false. And where ambiguities and controversies persist, who is meant to make the final decision? Who determines whether the plot is false or real? Who has more say? Or more power? This is not least true given that the uncertain cases are far more numerous than we ordinarily assume. Between the Watergate scandal and the incident at Roswell – the place where the bodies of extra-terrestrials are said to have been hidden after a flying saucer crashed – there is a wide range of plots, of greater or lesser real or imaginary character. In the long run, history often disproves hypotheses and judgements; the truth that emerges can overturn overly hasty verdicts. Not to mention that complex game of mirrors whereby pseudo-conspiracies cover up real ones, as in the trials that Stalin mounted against Trotsky and others between 1936 and 1938. Nor can it be forgotten that fictitious allegations of plots have not infrequently had very real and even devastating effects.[3]

If there are people obsessed with plots, it is because plots do indeed exist. A glaring case in point is what happened in the aftermath of 11 September 2001, when, in order to legitimise its otherwise completely illegitimate intervention in Iraq, the world's most prestigious democracy declared that Saddam Hussein possessed 'weapons of mass destruction' – and even tried to adduce evidence and documents for this claim. That was the 'official line' of the US administration, which was later contradicted and disavowed by the lack of any substantiation. Faced with such examples, how can we blame those who suspect the powerful of some ploy – that is, the powerful who, while discreetly covering up their own immoral conduct, plant the label of 'conspiracy theorists' on others?

In democratic countries, where transparency ought to have dispelled the shadow of the *arcana imperii*, the opposite has often been the case. The influence of the secret services, together with the ineptitude and failings of the judiciary, have prevented obscure and disturbing developments from reaching the light of day. The so-called matter of state has often become the tombstone over the truth. Emblematic of all this is the Italian context: from the 1960s onwards, it was marked by coup plots, falsehoods produced by the secret services, the collusion with the Mafia of parts of the state machine, and violence and neo-fascist bombs.[4] Even today, these events are still largely shrouded in mystery. As if to thicken the fog, conspiracist plots are attached to the actions of the Red Brigades, with the not too hidden agenda of delegitimising them. But also evident is the intent of downplaying the great uprising that took place on the left, perhaps the most important in the Western world in the post-war period. If in some areas this revolt degenerated into armed struggle, on the whole it had broad support behind it. But, in light of this past, what should citizens think of the democracy they live in? What trust should they have in institutions and what relationship with power? Does all this not fuel the belief that a plot is afoot?

In a short literary essay, where his well-known ironic verve comes to the fore, the writer Mordechai Richler has one of his interlocutors say: 'The trouble with conspiracy theories . . . is that so many of them have proved to be right. For years, I laughed at my left-wing friends when they told me their telephones were being tapped or that Nixon was a crook, and now, look, they were right all along.'[5]

Reducing the belief in plots to a pathological phenomenon, to a deviance that violates the norm of established truth, is completely counterproductive and, on the contrary, triggers the perverse mechanism of an endless spiral of doubt. The expert called upon to refute, with data and tables, the counter-expert on duty, increases suspicion, sharpens scepticism and *ressentiment*. This is why a fashionable disdain for conspiracism is a boomerang that serves only to deepen the rift between the high-mindedly conformist and the non-conformist. It is, then, unavoidable to assume that the former – i.e. those who see only legends and lies when it comes to doubts over the established powers – are always already on their side. Which is further proof for those who are distrustful.

On the other hand, the denunciation of plots afoot is itself a tool of power. It seems clear that, in recent decades, the state has resorted to it in ever-more refined fashion. As with terrorism, however, the state does not have a monopoly on legitimate accusation. And it cannot accuse others of being terrorists or conspiracists. Unless, that is, it wants to criminalise dissent, disavow criticism, and depoliticise any debate.

Anti-conspiracists also turn out to be obsessed with conspiracy – if only because they believe they see everywhere the long shadow of conspiracism. Frédéric Lordon has rightly noted that this happens precisely to the powerful, to those immersed in the machinery of power.[6] From this basis, they launch their anti-conspiracist crusades against the fake news of others, the false information of dissidents, the fables of popular paranoia.

However, if police-style denunciation is enough to disqualify itself, power is not going to be challenged with the epidemic of a thousand alternative truths. On the contrary, this means remaining stuck within the workings of power and helping them continue their onward grind. In other words, dooming oneself to impotence.

Precisely because conspiracism is a weapon of mass depoliticisation, a political reflection is needed that makes it easier to step away from this all-embracing explanatory scheme. As always, to understand is not to justify, nor does it entail any indulgence.

But we cannot fail to recognise that conspiracism stems from the fear and isolation of the citizen who feels excluded from the public space. Where the *pólis* has become inaccessible, where the interpretative community is shattered, the common truth is also shattered. There, the spectre of the plot lurks.

Notes

Who Pulls the Strings?

1 Pioneers include Norman Cohn, Leo Löwenthal, Richard Hofstadter, Serge Moscovici, Raoul Girardet and Léon Poliakov.
2 Rob Brotherton, *Suspicious Minds: Why We Believe Conspiracy Theories*. London: Bloomsbury, 2021.
3 Michael Butter, *'Nichts ist wie es scheint': Über Verschwörungstheorien*. Frankfurt am Main: Suhrkamp, 2018.
4 Translator's note: in Italian this is known as 'poteri forti', literally 'strong powers'. There is a certain overlap with the English-language idea of the 'Deep State' – those forces behind the scenes who 'really' hold power, in defiance of democratic choice – but it is not limited to the state machine per se, also extending to private enterprise, the media, and so on.

Politics and its Shadow-Realm

1 For an overview, see Jovan Byford, *Conspiracy Theories: A Critical Introduction*. New York: Palgrave Macmillan, 2015; Pierre-André Taguieff, *Les théories du complot*. Paris: Que sais-je?, 2021.

Enigmas and Misunderstandings

1 Paolo Prodi, *Il sacramento del potere: il giuramento politico nella storia costituzionale dell'Occidente*. Bologna: il Mulino, 1992.
2 Filippo Buonarroti, *Cospirazione per l'eguaglianza detta di Babeuf*, trans. Gastone Manacorda. Turin: Einaudi, [1928] 1971, p. 4; Eng. trans. as *Buonarroti's History of Babeuf's Conspiracy for Equality*. London: H. Hetherington, 1836.
3 Alex Butterworth, *The World That Never Was: A True Story of Dreamers, Schemers, Anarchists and Secret Agents*. New York: Vintage, 2011.
4 As shown by Luc Boltanski, who deconstructs established definitions like the one proposed by Peter Knight: Luc Boltanski, *Énigmes et complots: une enquête à propos d'enquêtes*. Paris: Gallimard, 2021, pp. 283–7; Peter Knight, 'Making sense of conspiracy theories', in *Conspiracy Theories in American History: An Encyclopedia*, 2 vols. Santa Barbara, CA: ABC-Clio, 2003, vol. I, p. 15.

The Workings of the Plot

1 Martin Heidegger, *The Question Concerning Technology*. New York: Garland, [1954] 1977; *Bremen and Freiburg Lectures*. Bloomington: Indiana University Press, 2012.
2 Giorgio Agamben, *Che cos'è un dispositivo*. Milan: Nottetempo, 2006; Eng. trans. as *What is an Apparatus? and Other Essays*. Stanford, CA: Stanford University Press, 2009.

Democracy and Power

1 François Furet, *Penser la Révolution française*. Paris: Gallimard, 1978, pp. 81ff.; Eng. trans. as *Interpreting the French Revolution*. Cambridge: Cambridge University Press, 1981.
2 Claude Lefort, 'The question of democracy', in *Democracy and Political Theory*. Cambridge: Polity, 1988, pp. 9–20.
3 Ibid., p. 17.
4 Jacques Rancière, *Hatred of Democracy*. London: Verso, 2005.

The Cause of All Our Ills

1 The classic work which explains the consequences it had was Norman Cohn, *Warrant for Genocide: The Myth of the Jewish World Conspiracy and the Protocols of the Elders of Zion.* London: Serif, [1966] 1996.
2 Léon Poliakov, *La causalité diabolique: essai sur l'origine des persécutions.* Paris: Calmann-Lévy, 1980, p. 11.
3 Manès Sperber, 'The police conception of history', in *The Achilles Heel.* New York: Doubleday, 1960.
4 Karl Popper, *The Open Society and its Enemies*, Vol. II: *The High Tide of Prophecy.* London: Routledge, [1945] 1969; *Conjectures and Refutations: The Growth of Scientific Knowledge.* London: Routledge, [1963] 2002.
5 Friedrich Nietzsche, *Beyond Good and Evil.* Cambridge: Cambridge University Press, [1886] 2001, p. 21.
6 Friedrich Nietzsche, *Twilight of the Idols.* Oxford: Oxford University Press, [1889] 1998.

Hungry for Myths

1 Mircea Eliade, *The Sacred and the Profane.* New York: Harcourt Press, 1959, p. 95.
2 Georges Sorel, *Reflections on Violence.* New York: Dover, [1908] 2012, p. 127.
3 Furio Jesi, *Materiali mitologici: mito e antropologia nella cultura europea*, ed. Andrea Cavalletti. Turin: Einaudi, 2001.
4 Theodore Ziolkowski, *Cults and Conspiracies: A Literary History.* Baltimore: Johns Hopkins University Press, 2013, pp. 159ff.

The Prague Cemetery

1 The three stories, given in italics, are drawn (and liberally rewritten) from Hermann O. F. Gödsche's novel *Biarritz*, as well as from the *Protocols*, from Eugène Sue's *The Wandering Jew*, and from Alexandre Dumas' *Cagliostro*.
2 On the uses of the *Protocols* in recent decades, especially in Arab countries, see André Taguieff, *L'imaginaire du complot mondial: aspects d'un mythe moderne.* Paris: Mille et une nuits, 2006, pp. 142ff. Another excellent guide is Will Eisner's *The Plot: The*

Secret Story of the Protocols of the Elders of Zion. New York: W. W. Norton, 2005.

Spokesmen for the Deceived

1 Richard Hofstadter, *The Paranoid Style in American Politics*. New York: Vintage, [1965] 2016.
2 Leo Löwenthal and Norbert Guterman, *Prophets of Deceit: A Study of the Techniques of the American Agitator*, intro. Alberto Toscano. London: Verso, [1949] 2021.
3 T. W. Adorno, with Else Frenkel-Brunswik, Daniel J. Levinson, and R. Nevitt Sanford, *The Authoritarian Personality*. London: Verso, [1950] 2021.

Sovereign *Ressentiment*

1 Friedrich Nietzsche, *On the Genealogy of Morals*. London: Continuum, [1887] 2008, Part I, §§ 10–15.
2 Marc Angenot, *Les idéologies du ressentiment*. Montreal: XYZ, 1997.
3 Max Scheler, *Ressentiment*. Milwaukee: Marquette, [1912–15] 2003.

The New World Order

1 Ernst Jünger, *Der Weltstaat*. Stuttgart: Klett, 1960.
2 Jacques Attali, *Demain, qui gouvernera le monde?* Paris: Fayard, 2011.
3 Paul Hanebrink, *A Specter Haunting Europe: The Myth of Judeo-Bolshevism*. Cambridge, MA: Belknap Press, 2018.
4 Johann Gottlieb Fichte, *Contribution to the Correction of the Public's Judgments on the French Revolution*. New York: State University of New York Press, [1793] 2021.
5 See Serdar Kaya, 'The rise and decline of the Turkish 'Deep State': the Ergenekon case', in *Insight Turkey*, XI/4 (2009), pp. 9–13. On this concept, see Gérald Bronner, 'L'état profond, c'est la stigmatisation du caractère illusoire supposé du monde, et du pouvoir en particulier', *L'Opinion*, 22 July 2020, www.lopinion .fr/economie/gerald-bronner-letat-profond-cest-la-stigmatisation -du-caractere-illusoire-suppose-du-monde-et-du-pouvoir-en-par ticulier.

6 See Max Weber, *Economy and Society*. Cambridge, MA: Harvard University Press, [1922] 2019.

The 'Great Replacement' and the QAnon Patriots

1 But no less disturbing were reports of a survey conducted in France in 2017 by the Fondation Jean-Jaurès and the Observatoire du conspirationnisme, according to which almost half of respondents agreed that immigration is 'a political project to replace one civilisation with another, deliberately organized by political, intellectual and media elites, which should be ended by sending those peoples back where they came from' (see www.ifop.com /wp-content/uploads/2018/03/3942-1-study_file.pdf).
2 See Valérie Igounet and Rudy Reichstadt, 'Le "Grand Remplacement" est-il un concept complotiste?', September 2018, https://jean-jaures.org/nos-productions/le-grand-remplacement -est-il-un-concept-complotiste.
3 See Adolf Hitler, *Mein Kampf*, [1925], chapter 'State member vs. state citizen'.
4 See Ingrid Walker, 'White hope: conspiracy, nationalism, and revolution in *The Turner Diaries* and *Hunter*', in Peter Knight (ed.), *Conspiracy Nation: The Politics of Paranoia in Postwar America*. New York: New York University Press, 2002, pp. 157–76.
5 Other attacks linked to this book include the one in Oklahoma City in 1995.

The Extreme Taste for the Apocalypse

1 Norman Cohn, *The Pursuit of the Millennium: Revolutionary Millenarians and Mystical Anarchists of the Middle Ages*. Oxford: Oxford University Press, 1970.
2 Raoul Girardet, *Mythes et mythologies politiques*. Paris: Seuil, 1986, pp. 44ff.
3 Philippe Burrin, *Nazi Anti-Semitism: From Prejudice to the Holocaust*. New York: W. W. Norton, 2005; see also Donatella Di Cesare, 'Antisemitismo', in *Enciclopedia Treccani: lessico del XXI secolo*, Rome: Istituto dell'Enciclopedia Treccani, 2021, pp. 61–6.

Populism and the Plot

1 Cas Mudde and Cristobal Rovira Kaltwasser, *Populism: A Very Short Introduction*. Oxford: Oxford University Press, 2017.
2 Ernesto Laclau, *On Populist Reason*. London: Verso, 2005.
3 Pierre-André Taguieff, *L'illusion populiste: essai sur les démagogies de l'âge démocratique*. Paris: Flammarion, 2007.
4 See Russell Muirhead and Nancy L. Rosenblum, *A Lot of People Are Saying: The New Conspiracism and the Assault on Democracy*. Princeton, NJ: Princeton University Press, 2019, pp. 62ff.

Victimhood and Political Powerlessness

1 See Fredric Jameson, 'Cognitive mapping', in C. Nelson and L. Grossberg (eds), *Marxism and Interpretation of Culture*. London: Macmillan, 1988, p. 356; see also Fran Mason, 'A poor person's cognitive mapping', in Peter Knight (ed.), *Conspiracy Nation: The Politics of Paranoia in Postwar America*. New York: New York University Press, 2002, pp. 40–56.

On the 'Heresy' of Believers in Plots

1 Umberto Eco, *I limiti dell'interpretazione*. Milan: La nave di Teseo, [1990] 2016, pp. 59ff.; Eng. trans. as *The Limits of Interpretation*. Bloomington: Indiana University Press, 1994.
2 See Umberto Eco, *Foucault's Pendulum*. New York: Ballantine, 1997.
3 Eco, *I limiti dell'interpretazione*, p. 68.

Transparency and Secrecy

1 Georg Simmel, 'The secret and the secret society', in *Sociology: Inquiries into the Construction of Social Forms*. Glencoe, IL: Free Press, 1950, p. 332.
2 Marc Bloch, *The Historian's Craft*. Manchester: Manchester University Press, 1992, p. 66.
3 Theodor Adorno, 'Theses against occultism', in *Minima Moralia*. London: Verso, 1974, pp. 238–44.
4 On Assange and his choices, see Donatella di Cesare, *The Time of Revolt*. Cambridge: Polity, 2021, pp. 110–17.

5 See Stanley Fish, '"Transparency" is the mother of fake news', *New York Times*, 7 May 2018, www.nytimes.com/2018/05/07/opinion/transparency-fake-news.html.

In Praise of Suspicion

1 Friedrich Nietzsche, *The Will to Power*. New York: Random House, 1967, p. 327.
2 Martin Parker, 'Human science as conspiracy theory', in Jane Parish and Martin Parker (eds), *The Age of Anxiety: Conspiracy Theory and the Human Sciences*. Oxford: Blackwell, 2001, pp. 191–207.
3 Fredric Jameson also partly moves in this direction, though his intentions are rather different.
4 Bruno Latour, 'Why has critique run out of steam? From matters of facts to matters of concern', *Critical Inquiry*, 30/2 (2004), p. 230.
5 Luc Boltanski, *Énigmes et complots: une enquête à propos d'enquêtes*. Paris: Gallimard, 2021, p. 319.
6 Paul Ricoeur, *Freud and Philosophy: An Essay on Interpretation*. New Haven, CT: Yale University Press, 1970.

Beyond Anti-Conspiracism

1 See Ginna Husting and Martin Ott, 'Dangerous machinery: "Conspiracy theorist" as a transpersonal strategy of exclusion', *Symbolic Interaction*, 30/2 (2007): 127–50.
2 See Noam Chomsky, *9/11: Institutional Analysis vs. Conspiracy Theory*, Z Blogs, 6 October 2006. https://znetwork.org/zblogs/9-11-institutional-analysis-vs-conspiracy-theory-by-noam-chomsky/.
3 Carlo Ginzburg, *Il filo e le tracce: vero falso finto*. Milan: Feltrinelli, 2006, pp. 301ff.; Eng. trans. as *Threads and Traces: True, False, Fictive*. Berkeley: University of California Press, 2012.
4 On this climate, see Carlo Ginzburg, *Il giudice e lo storico: considerazioni in margine al processo Sofri*. 2nd edn, Macerata: Quodlibet, [1991] 2020.
5 Mordechai Richler, *Broadsides: Reviews and Opinions*. New York: Viking, 1990, p. 56.
6 Frédéric Lordon, 'Le complotisme de l'anticomplotisme', *Le Monde diplomatique*, October 2017, www.monde-diplomatique.fr/20.